Principles of 21ˢᵗ Century Governance

Journey to High Performance Boards

Les Wallace, Ph.D.

Les Wallace, Ph.D.
President
Signature Resources Inc.
PO Box 460100
Aurora, CO 80046

Les@signatureresources.com

www.signatureresources.com
21st Century Governance

Library of Congress Cataloging-in-Publication Data

Wallace, Les
Principles of 21st Century Governance/Les Wallace
Includes bibliographical references
ISBN-13: 9781493536900
ISBN-10: 1493536907

Dedication

To the thousands of board members who have participated in my governance seminars and helped me frame, polish and communicate principles of high performance governance.

Acknowledgments

Special gratitude to my family Connie, Amy and Scott, Katy and Scott, Emerson and Hayden who endured long hours of writing and editing during family visits to our Colorado cabin.

Special thanks to long term professional associates and friends Dennis Phillips, Kathy Hanson, Christy Crosser, and Larry Goldstein who have helped me shape a consulting presence and upon whom I can still consistently rely to tell me when I might be off base.

Contents

Preface

"The problem is never how to get new innovative thoughts into your mind, but how to get the old ones out." Dee Hoc

It's time to change the conversation about your governance model. From my service on boards of directors and while providing governance development work with over 300 boards of directors and thousands of board members I've evolved strong feelings about what constitutes high performance governance. Customer feedback on my presentations and on-site development work and reader feedback on my published articles has encouraged me to keep pushing for a next generation of high performance governance. While watching boards work and accumulating guidance to boards for over 30 years, I've frequently been asked to pull my thoughts, articles and guidance together in a way that might serve as a governance primer—concise, easily read, and addressing some of the most challenging or most overlooked elements of effective governance.

Principles of 21st Century Governance is not intended to be a comprehensive treatise on effective governance. For that I suggest four excellent sources that provide far more comprehensive thought on elements of governance: John Carver, Boards that make a Difference (1996); Richard Chiat, et. al., Governance as Leadership (2004); The Source: Twelve Principles of Governance that Power Exceptional Boards (BoardSource 2005), and Ram Charan, Owning Up: The 14 Questions Every Board Member Needs to Ask (2009).

Principles of 21st Century Governance is intended to support boards of directors from the most inexperienced local boards to the most sophisticated international governing bodies. I believe it stands alone, without my support, to set the table about what governance should look like and incite board discussion toward growing better governance. I've addressed some of the most basic elements of governance while also trying to stretch our thinking about what governance should look like in this century—a century where the future is coming at us faster, with more complexity and in a manner that is forcing boards of directors to attend differently to their important responsibilities.

I dedicate this work to all the board chairpersons and CEOs who have had the courage to invite me into their governance sanctuary with the openness to be challenged about what excellence in governance should look like. They knew, everyone of them, that I would not hesitate to point out their ugly babies nor hesitate setting the bar much higher for their governance model.

In my leadership book co-authored with Dr. Jim Trinka, A Legacy of 21st Century Leadership (2007) we pointed out that leaders in this century needed to begin changing the conversation about what leadership is and how leadership impacts sustainable legacies for their enterprise. That's the primary charge I give to you as board member—begin the conversation about how your governance needs to change to be relevant in the turbulence of the 21st Century. Remember this about board service—"the organization doesn't owe you anything for your volunteer board effort." You've chosen to be a trustee out of a service commitment so commit to legacy or move on.

Les Wallace, Ph.D.
Aurora, Colorado
les@signatureresources.com

CHAPTER 1

From Governance to Governance Leadership

"A successful board governs its company by continually challenging every significant facet of its operations—business model, strategies and underlying assumptions, operating performance and leadership development." Bonnie Gwin (2010)

The signals of the early 21ˢᵗ Century indicate a next generation of governance sophistication and practice may be necessary. In this century the implications of globalization have touched every organization, community and government on the planet and the connectedness is accelerating rather than retreating. The 21ˢᵗ Century dawned as an angry, hydra-headed economic monster, wreaking damage that may take decades to heal and will likely change financial and governmental behavior for decades more. Increasing demands from customers and citizens, heightened expectations for the innovation required to compete and the dual impacts of baby boomers leaving the workforce as Millennials enter it are creating entirely new forks in the road. Then there's global climate change, and whatever our point of view, we must admit it still poses multiple dilemmas for us all.

Policy governance is a solid foundation for boards but insufficient to define high performance governance in today's world. While some boards still struggle to achieve a "policy based" approach to governance, other boards are adapting quickly to the dynamics of the 21ˢᵗ Century by moving to what I call a "governance leadership" model. The next few pages briefly contrast the two and suggest some of the markers your board might use to determine if they've arrived at the next level of governance excellence.

Policy Governance

Most boards, and especially new board members, struggle with over-managing their enterprises. The less governance-experienced member dives into operational detail with relish and strives to dictate tactical events of the organization rather than sticking to policy and strategy guidance. John Carver (Boards that make a Difference, 2006) addressed this micro-managing tendency by defining the "policy governance model" to help boards focus on leading the organization and letting the CEO manage.

Thousands of boards have benefited by using the Carver model to upgrade their governance conversations around policy development, focusing on results, ethics, CEO leadership and self-assessment. While consent agendas and regular board self assessment may still not be average fare for all boards, the Carver model is prominent in the governance literature and training programs across enterprise governance segments worldwide.

Conversations of a typical policy based governing meeting focus on fiduciary oversight of organizational performance, policy review and creation, customer, member, constituent satisfaction, CEO performance and annual planning processes. Typical reports from the CEO and finance department are pages in length and discussed fairly extensively by the board. Annual cycles cue up key policy areas for board review (purchasing, human resources, benefits, customer treatment, etc.). These boards also frequently reserve a weekend per year to consider the annual planning process and refresh their long-range plan.

Governance Leadership

More than ten years ago Peter Vaill (Vaill, 1996) used a river metaphor to warn that the cycle of rapids and calm we had known in the past was becoming "permanent whitewater." He was right, and the implications are pretty straightforward. They echo in most major management, leadership and governance publications around the globe: *organizations must transform, not simply change, and they must drive transformation rather than react to it.*

We must think more strategically than ever before and become much more sensitive sentinels of the business environment surrounding our enterprises. That means creating many more leaders than followers, and anticipating leadership needs rather than hoping to find help when the need arises.

We must navigate these whitewater rapids with greater integrity and transparency than ever before, because dishonesty and greed remain aggressive, not simply opportunistic. In the business community the early 21st Century is known as the "new normal."

Dimensions of a Governance Leadership Model

The governance leadership model increases conversations around strategic thinking and organizational transformation. Boards focus up to 75 percent of their discussion time at every meeting anticipating the future through regular conversations about the changing business environment. They manage traditional fiduciary and policy conversations more effectively and efficiently to allow more time for strategic discourse.

The governance leadership model sets the table for timely organizational corrections in the event that certain strategies begin to falter. The model helps boards drive real innovation rather than mere tinkering with products and business models. Governance leadership fosters transparency, both internal and external, and guides the different sorts of conversations, policies, and boundary management such transparency requires.

A governance leadership model facilitates board leadership succession through a longitudinal effort, pre-dating board appointments by several years. It enables boards to develop higher levels of leadership, beyond simple management, at all tiers of the organization. Its inclusive intelligence listens to the amplified voices of critics and customers on the cusp of innovative expectations, and tracks customer value, not simply customer satisfaction.

Implications for Your Board of Directors

It's hard work to be exceptional. Most boards are not exceptional and when their organizations gain any degree of success it can lull them into complacency, dull their development, and distract them from grooming the next generation of governance talent. Tom Friedman warned us (The World is Flat, 2005) that "change is hard—it's hardest on those caught by surprise."

Therein lies the premise behind a governance leadership model. Driven by a "culture of inquiry," the governance leadership model is not likely to let change catch it by surprise. The model focuses as much dialogue as possible on thinking in the "future tense" at every meeting—not simply at the annual retreat.

Looking at characteristics of policy governance and governance leadership side by side may help you determine the implications for your board's governance development [Table 1].

"Governance leadership comes alive in the give and take among board members. If this dialogue is relegated to a stopwatch type mentality, or worse yet, filled by staff and consultant PowerPoint™ presentations that limit time for questions and board dialogue, then your board is missing the 21ˢᵗ Century benchmark."

TABLE 1

Policy-Based Governance *Organizational performance oversight*	Governance Leadership *Future-facing conversations*
Fiduciary and policy-based discussions take up 75 percent of board conversations.	*Fiduciary and policy-based governance is reduced to 25–50 percent of board conversations.*
■ Fiduciary conversations.*	*Governance Leadership drives 50–75 percent of Board conversations each meeting, e.g.:*
■ CEO performance oversight.	
■ Staff update presentations.	■ *Environmental scanning and tracking.*
■ Customer satisfaction review.	■ *Strategic thinking about transformation.*
■ Policy review and creation.	■ *Scenario building.*
■ Periodic self-assessment.	■ *Strategic plan review (5 year horizon).*
■ Annual planning processes.	■ *Innovation and breakthrough discussion.*
	■ *Benchmarking with innovators.*
	■ *Dissecting best practice models within and outside the industry.*
	■ *Purposeful transparency.*
	■ *Board leadership succession.*
	■ *Organizational leadership succession.*
	■ *Inclusive customer input data.*
	■ *Customer value tracking (not simply satisfaction).*
*See Chapter 3 for more detail on fiduciary responsibility.	■ *Annual self-assessment and development plan.*

Typical Governance Leadership Board Meeting

To protect time for forward-facing conversations, boards using the governance leadership model use **consent agendas** and **exception reports** to keep meeting time spent on oversight and update matters to approximately 25-50 percent.

Using consent agendas cuts through standard reports (such as the CEO's report) and common board actions (like approving the updating of authorization signatures). A more advanced board may use the Internet to review the consent agenda and other reports electronically before the meeting. Board members may approve the items or request an item be pulled for full board discussion. Typically, it is unnecessary to pull an item for review unless it presents new developments or unwanted, unexpected variations. The Board then presents the on-line actions for formal approval during a live board session.

For important fiduciary items like **financial reports**, the committee or executive (CFO, finance committee, or audit committee) presents an exception report describing variations from the approved budget or accounting principals. This is similar to the way boards review the annual external audit by focusing on the auditor's "exceptions" or "cautions" but not discussing the entire report, which they should have reviewed in advance.

There is no need for a full and complete review of the balance sheet and budget variations at every meeting. Gone are the tedious, page by page, scratching and sniffing of six pages of financial report numbers—that job should have been delegated to a committee. Only those elements the committee or officer deem a significant exception must be called to the attention of the board for due diligence. The board then discusses and takes appropriate action or accepts and duly notes the report into the record. Of course, any board member who has serious reservation about the completeness of the committee's scrutiny can call for discussion of other financial reporting items.

High Performance Board Meetings

Board dialogue about strategy is more urgent than ever. High performance boards attempt to reserve 50-75 percent of their agenda for strategic action and discussion, such as taking stock of their **strategic plan**, visiting new developments in their external environment, or stretching their strategic thinking toward higher-risk innovations. Frequently a board will revisit one strategic initiative per meeting or the Chair and CEO will place a business environment update (for external awareness) on the agenda for discussion.

Other forward-facing conversations include **leadership succession** (discussed at least twice a year), customer value tracking data (discussed two to four times a year), **board self-assessment and development** issues (again, forward facing), and **benchmarking innovative practices** in the organization's field.

The bottom line difference between typical boards and high performance boards is that progressive boards refine and focus traditional oversight conversations to create efficiencies that can be re-invested in strategic issues.

Your board may be closer than you think to the time investments recommended here—look at the minutes from your last six board meetings and compare. However, consider not simply the time spent in board action, but also the time spent in board dialogue, or, what one expert calls "generative thinking" (Chiat, et. al., <u>Governance as Leadership</u>, 2005). Governance leadership comes alive in the give and take among board members. If this generative dialogue is relegated to a stopwatch type mentality, or worse yet, filled by staff and consultant PowerPoint™ presentations that limit time for questions and board dialogue, then your board is missing the 21st Century benchmark.

"If I may I'd like to gripe about something completely unrelated..."

Managing the Board's Time: Weeds, Positioning and Discipline

Time is one of the most scarce board resources. Unless yours is an exceptional board, the meeting conversations you typically have could benefit from refinement and focus. For example, typical boards might dig into the weeds of the CEO's report, the new marketing plan or the financial report. Assuming your enterprise is stable and not in operational or financial crisis, this behavior is excessive and unnecessary for effective governance. Effective use of committees, external review (auditors) and focused reports to the board can answer most of the questions that take up airtime at your meeting. And, many of these can be read and digested in advance of board meetings so oral "report outs" are not necessary.

Overcoming Board Groupthink

From 1970s research on small group decision-making came the concept anyone who has worked with groups can recognize—"group think." Groupthink can occur in a board of directors when the desire for harmony or group complacency regarding the issue results in failing to adequately appraise the data and alternatives. It can also occur with groups who don't wish to disagree with the Chair or CEO and trust rather than speak up. Whatever the cause, group think diminishes the duty of care—using your best judgment and applying standards of reasonableness and prudence. Agreed upon rules of engagement can help a board never have to worry about group think—try these on.

- **Benchmarking**. No proposal should be brought to the board for a new policy, product or service without also bringing along marketplace intelligence about what others have done. There are very few "new" ideas in the business so its quite likely some organization somewhere has already traveled this road. Find out what the most successful organizations came up with and discuss it relative to your situation.

  Benchmarking can also include gathering internal feedback from key staff who are closest to the idea, product, service, policy or procedure. You've hired good people so let's hear from those on the ground who may be closest to the reality. We know your CEO is bright but inclusive perspectives are the gold standard of decision making in the 21st Century.

- **Honor the hard question**. Instead of responding to the hard questions with something like "that doesn't apply here" or "I think we already have sufficient data," say instead—"tell me more about why you ask?" "What are you skeptical, fearful of or unclear about?" This more appreciative approach to disagreement frequently creates learning rather than conflict.

- **Use paradigm-shifting questions**. "What would our younger members think of this decision?" "What will our employees think of this policy, procedure?" "What might it take to make this a no risk proposition?" "What key metrics will we use to track the success of this decision?"

- **Always review the basic questions**. Is this in line with our core values? Mission? Vision? Risk appetite? Make answers to these questions part of the proposal for consideration in order to force the board's attention.

- **Time**. The bigger the risk of an idea or proposal the more time should be spent in dialogue and reflection. Possibly introduce and discuss the concept at one meeting and re-visit it at the next meeting. Neuroscientists verify that sleeping on big questions and risks helps the mind focus and can lead to different questions and perspectives.

- **Forced Participation.** Our trusteeship to our customers, members and constituents is far too big a responsibility to let high stakes discussions take place without hearing from everyone. Call on the silent board members. Ask them specific questions: "What concerns you the most?" "Do you feel you have enough information?" "If this decision shows up in the news headlines tomorrow will you be comfortable?" The roots of groupthink begin with not including everyone. Force it if you must. Watch for non-verbal signs of withdrawal or discomfort and ask the person about it.

- **Listen to the buzz**. I tell boards that conversation on issues should take place in the boardroom not the hallways. Such is the behavior of professionals but we don't always have experienced professionals on our boards. The hallway, bathroom or smoking stoop talk can be signs that all's not in sync with the board. Pay particular attention to this murmur as a sign you still have some dialogue left to pursue.

- **Quick course corrections**. Every leadership book ever written suggests that authentic leaders are not afraid to say, "oops." Facing less than optimum decisions head on when the evidence starts to add up is healthy not weak. Just like no battle plan every survived the first shot on the battlefield without re-calibration, so too goes governance decision-making.

When an abnormal temperature of a decision or the aches and chills set in, listen to your instinct and ask to revisit the decision. If you're doing this with every big decision then maybe you should revisit your evidence based decision-making process. But inevitably, even the best board will be forced to look in the mirror and say—that wasn't optimal, let's correct it. The implication here is that you should always ask two more questions of the highest risk decisions: What will be the early signs of success or failure? "What's our contingency plan?"

> *The future is aging faster and faster, dealing us new wild cards every day. Many experts are deeming this chaos the "new normal." Assuming reasonable operational and financial health of your organization, in the new normal, your most important governance contributions are positioning and repositioning the enterprise and your board.*

So how do you move your board work to a more strategic "governance leadership" mode? With self-assessment, purpose and discipline. We have seen some boards make this move in the span of a few meetings while others make a journey over several years. The boards that made the transition quickly recognized that their less sophisticated members, the ones who still wished to manage the organization, were holding them back. They developed a strategy for leadership succession to attract more competent board members.

Having witnessed many boards struggle with maturing their governance beyond simple oversight to more future-based conversations we can only say you will make no movement unless you open the conversation. You might start by using the set of "High Performance Governance Indicators" in Chapter 2 to check your progress and begin a dialogue.

The Best Board Meeting I Ever Attended

The executive in charge of board development for a large national philan-thropic organization, with over a hundred regional boards, recently asked me, "What's the best board meeting you ever attended?" Got me to thinking...no, it wasn't chaired by me. Yes, it was one of my clients. Here's what it looked like.

Consent agenda. The monthly meeting began with approval of the consent agenda—online and prior to the physical board meeting. This included the CEO report and several updates from key staff members. Proper use of the consent agenda moved dialogue to the more vital issues rather than unnecessary discussion of the common trivial data inherent in any board packet.

Important to trivial. The most important business and strategic issues were first on the formal agenda and the rest in descending order—no more "old business" "new business" structure. Yes, it appears a bit radical and divergent from "Robert's Rules of Order." However, those "rules" are ancient history to today's high performance board of directors.

Dashboard financials. The financial report—the first business item on the agenda—was presented as a one-page dashboard of key financial indi-cators that the board had developed a couple of years ago (color coded green, yellow, red). This "at-a-glance" approach allowed the board to scan the identified key indicators for monthly and year-to-date performance to budget as well as a past year comparison. The dashboard confirmed no exceptions to the monthly financials, was motioned to be attached to the minutes by the finance committee chair, and documented in the minutes.

Attending to board succession. A "Governance Leadership Succession" agenda item followed with a discussion of the cadre of potential future board members (10) the board had engaged. Conversation focused on the three that were top candidates for the upcoming two board openings nine months hence and how they fit the desired board make-up profile. I had conducted a special educational session at their last board retreat on how to go about this due diligence and they were now tracking quarterly progress on early identification and development of next generation board members.

Reduced trivial jibber-jabber. Board members had read the board packet and their contributions were cogent and to the issue. No repeating what other board members had said. No drifting off into administrivia—they kept a hard focus on the matters at hand and a soft focus on dealing with one another. Through self-assessment and governance coaching they had learned to quiet the unnecessary trivial chatter and redundant comments that seeps into less disciplined meetings. They saved space for meaningful dialogue later during the "strategic update" segment of the meeting which accounts for 50 to 75 percent of meeting time in high performance governance.

Executive summaries. Staff and committee presentations and recommendations were in "executive summary" one page format—background information had been provided on the board section of the web site for those who wished more detailed information. This jump-started the board discussion on action verses the history of how we got there. The executive summaries included a highlight of key historical points and a couple of typical frequently asked questions relevant to governance decision making. An executive summary approach to reports can be expected to cut substantial board deliberation time by assuring you get to the point and don't waste time on irrelevant curiosity about benign details. [See more on "Executive Briefings" and "Executive Summaries" in the Support Materials section]

75 percent strategic dialogue. Thirty minutes into the agenda "business oversight" (fiduciary accountability) was completed and the board moved on to update a significant strategic issue. This allowed substantial exploration of the continued relevance of the strategy, updates on progress, new data points and information relative to the strategy, confirmation of continued importance and recommitment to tactics, timing and resources. This conversation was "generative" in that it focused on creation of ideas and development of new perspectives on strategy. This is where the board had time for expansive dialogue (not simply discussion) which assured more thorough understanding and creative input. Remember the time saved by the consent agenda (+/- ten minutes for most boards), the financial dashboard and exception reporting (+/- fifteen minutes saved for most boards) and those "executive summaries" causing conversation to jump-start in decision mode (saving another estimated fifteen minutes for this board)— that time came in handy reinvested in rigorous strategic dialogue. At this meeting the strategic dialogue totaled sixty minutes and left the board feeling confident they were properly transforming to remain relevant and thinking in the future tense about their enterprise.

Board development. A short board development segment on enterprise risk management ended the meeting. Discussion focused on a governance article the board had read in advance. This fifteen minute segment of the agenda directly related to board development goals established during the annual strategic planning retreat based on their most recent annual governance self assessment. This board commits board development time to every agenda—sometimes separate as with this meeting or, frequently embedded in the "strategic review" segment of the agenda.

Pre-work. Good meetings not only require a disciplined approach they require adequate preparation. The board chairperson, vice-chairperson and CEO, and COO had met two weeks prior to the meeting to go over the proposed agenda and requisite background material the board might need. Ten calendar days prior to the meeting the "on-line" consent agenda vote occurred and the board also received their complete board packet including links to their "board only" web site where more detailed reports and background information were available for those interested.

Immediate assessment. Finally, using an old process from good meetings practices, each board member completed a quick evaluation survey of the meeting answering three open-ended questions: 1. Are you leaving the meeting confident in the overall performance of our organization? 2. Did you feel you had ample opportunity for input? 3. Would you change anything for future meetings?

Meeting frequency. This board meets each month so it's easier for them to keep current and manage a tight agenda. Next year they will experiment with two virtual board meetings where they will only focus on fiduciary oversight. They are contemplating this will be a thirty minute conference call with web based support. Other boards who meet quarterly may find it more challenging to achieve the agenda and strategy balance of this board but it can be done. It simply takes discipline and will.

Your board? Make this the year you reflect on the best meeting of the year and what made it so. If you're doing some quick assessment after every meeting you will enter a virtuous process of continual improvement that may make this year much better than last.

Reflection

What was your board's best meeting this year?

What made it so and have you been able to sustain that approach?

What might you target this coming year to scrub your meetings for efficiencies and give them a complete makeover?

The Context of a Policy and Strategy Governance Model

"The days of simply keeping close watch on operational policy as a governance model are over. Both a policy and strategy focus comprise the primary challenge of governing in the 21st Century."

In the 21st Century the primary challenge of governing includes a focus on both policy and strategy. Boards must gain competencies in these areas, especially in light of new, intense pressure around organizational integrity and organizational transformation. 21st Century governance thinks and acts strategically about the future of the enterprise. By leading the organization and CEO rather than micro-managing, 21st Century boards are able to maintain close oversight on ethical practices and reduce sophomoric skirmishes over the details of management operations.

A post Enron era brought on the Sarbanes Oxley Act, and the global financial meltdown of 2008 resulted in even greater scrutiny of financial performance for both private sector and not-for-profit organizations. External and internal auditing, financial policy, and board investment in oversight responsibilities stretch many boards unaccustomed to needing such financial literacy. If you govern in a highly regulated business domain the increased board attention to this oversight has demanded more time on your learning and discussion agenda.

Not-for-profit organizations have generally lagged private sector organizations in innovation of services, transformation of the enterprise, and strategic thinking and planning. However, as the pace of change and continued pressure for limited funding sources intensifies, not-for-profit boards must adapt by thinking and acting much more strategically. The days of evolutionary change have given way to revolutionary pressures challenging many boards without experience or leadership competencies to keep up. Within this challenge, getting the board's agreement on a clearly articulated governance model and a guiding set of principles represents important priorities for the journey to high-performance governance.

Even in the 20th Century, it was not uncommon for boards of directors to struggle with questions about their role. Boards have historically been comprised of members with more experience in management and organizational leadership than governance leadership. Their leadership experience has likely been more hands on than strategic; that is, more about the day-to-day decisions for tactics and problem solving than the broad, strategic directions and vision of the enterprise. As a result, such board members tend to stray into operational or tactical decisions that are the purview of management.

It's also not uncommon, when board positions rotate, for new members to have questions regarding organizational direction or processes. Especially in boards where members are "elected," running on a platform of change is common and can lead to some political sorting out of the basic questions of governance, such as, do we have sound policy, a realistic yet forward-reaching strategy and a governance model we use consistently?

Of course there are also political challenges to board participation. Some members who are dissatisfied with the actions of the organization may choose to ask management questions as an attempt to steer the organization and influence the day-to-day decisions of the CEO / Executive Director.

General board accountabilities

A quick review of general board accountabilities may help establish a context for policy and strategy governance.

- Your **mission** (why you exist) is to provide value and positive impact for a constituent community (customers, members, other constituents).

- Your **vision** (where you're going) identifies the new horizon of organizational impact you seek to stay relevant amid shifting marketplace dynamics.

- Your **values** are the standards of conduct to which you commit your organizational practices.

- Your **legal responsibilities** include fiduciary accountability to advance the mission and oversee assets in a responsible manner while attending to ethical corporate behavior.

- Your **role as a board member** is to make policy and strategy decisions, ensure operational systems accomplish your plans, and monitor details of organizational performance making course corrections and refreshing strategy as needed.

- Your **role as a committee member** is to monitor and assess governance functions to which you have been charged and to consider current and future issues and deliver advice to the full board.

- Your **measures**:
  - ~ Business success (traditional business measures relevant to your mission success).
  - ~ Customer, member, constituent satisfaction and value (traditional customer measures).

~   Staff engagement (positive organizational climate with high levels of employee engagement).

CHAPTER 2

High Performance Governance Indicators

High performance governance requires a complex alignment of board member competency, smart execution of governance principles and a commitment to keep improving. High performance governance board members are independent and accountable to processes that are ethical, effective, efficient, strategic and responsive to their constituency. In high performance governance settings board members are also governance competent—not simply professional experts in a specific domain such as finance, marketing or fundraising. Governance competency is a much broader portfolio of awareness, knowledge and ability to lead processes of enterprise oversight and future movement far beyond the typical management and executive experiences many of us have.

Like most competencies, governance competencies can be learned. If a board is lucky, these competencies are studied and learned prior to accepting a board appointment or election. **In the near future we are likely to see "pre-credentialing" of some basic level of governance competency to qualify for a board appointment.** Because I have seen so many volunteer and paid board members struggle with an appropriate governance role I strongly favor pre-credentialing!

As a potential board member or a current board member, check the following components of high performance governance as I see them and then decide: am I ready for the Boardroom? Is our board meeting these standards?

Some Governance Basics

- First things first...the organizational house is in order rather than disarray.

- Our mission is clear and organizational activities are aligned and achieving expectations of which we can be proud.

- Our financial health is stable and an ample six to twelve month operating reserve exists.

- Our governance practices meet the highest standards of individual and organizational integrity.

- We have a strong Finance Committee and separate Audit and Enterprise Risk Management Committee.

- Our executive team is leadership competent and has board confidence.

- Our by-laws, policies, and procedures are up to date (reviewed on a two to three-year calendar).

- Significant customer, member or constituent input assures that our goals and strategies remain relevant and supported by our constituency.

- Our constituent support (customer base, members, constituents) is stable if not growing.

- We have highly competent constituents available for and interested in board service.

Reflection

Is the board confident in the stability and performance around these basics?

Does the information and data flowing to the board assure you can confirm this performance?

Board Competency

- We have board job descriptions that clearly identify leadership competencies required for service. Our nominations and applications process and candidate forums are designed to confirm and explore these competencies.

- Term limits for both officers and board appointments assure board turnover and infusion of fresh perspectives.

- We have a governance leadership succession program in place to identify and develop future leaders from the field as early as two to five years before we might need them to serve.

- We select outside board members based on competency rather than emeritus status.

- Board members failing the involvement, attendance or conduct standards are removed for cause.

- Meeting agendas are strategic and high priority focused versus heavily operational and activity based.

- A balanced scorecard "dashboard" provides efficient oversight of key performance indicators, prevents information overload and helps our board stay out of the operational weeds.

- Annual self-assessments and development plans drive board development.

- All committees and task forces have written charters with outcomes and deliverables clearly identified.

25

Strategic

- 75 percent of our typical board agenda is devoted to strategic topics—future facing discussion.

- An up-to-date strategic plan is in place looking three to five years out.

- The board commits to refreshing the strategic plan annually.

- We have facilitated inclusive input from constituent leaders on the strategic plan (past board members, professional thought leaders, focus groups, potential board members in our succession pipeline, other groups of professionals who know our business and our mission, external experts).

Constituent Focus

- Twice a year, we conduct checks on customer, member, or constituent value and satisfaction (two different issues).   Satisfaction   =   "Happy with service and delivery." Value = "Your offerings meet my needs."

- Our board voice represents the broad spectrum of customer, member, or constituent interests vs narrow agendas.

- A robust and open communication strategy links constituent groups to the organization.

- Constituent engagement pathways represent a "buffet" of options allowing individualized choice (unbundled vs bundled).

Transparent and Dialogic Tone

- An unrushed board agenda assuring generative dialogue comprises 50 to 75 percent of the meeting.

- Board meetings are characterized by candid discussions with appreciative respect for diverse points of view.

- We are transparent with no back room agendas and limited use of "executive" or closed sessions.

- We make robust information available to constituents through a dynamic website, social media and our publications.

- We are making greater use of virtual meetings for committees and boards, to reduce travel commitments and expense.

Clarity in Direction to Executive Team

- There is alignment between the board and Executive Director or CEO on goals and performance.

- Twice a year, the board provides formal performance feedback to the Executive Director or CEO in the form of a brief mid-year and a full annual review.

- Executive Director or CEO and key staff reports are based on strategic outcomes and exceptions vs activities and administrative details.

Reflection

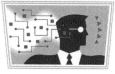

Which of these components of high performance governance caught your attention the most?

How might your board begin the dialogue about next generation governance leadership using these components as a starting point?

CHAPTER 3

The Role of Governance

"The role of the board of directors is to create, authorize and monitor the strategic direction for the enterprise. The board creates and approves values, policy and financial plans that support vibrant and sustained delivery on the mission. In general, governance sets the direction and approves the broad parameters within which the organization will perform. The CEO makes the management decisions necessary to deliver on policy and strategy direction."

The role of governance for a board of directors is to create, authorize and monitor the strategic direction of the enterprise and create values, policy and financial plans that support vibrant and sustained delivery on the mission.

The board hires an executive to make the decisions required to field a team, deliver on the organization's mission, and assure progress toward the strategic objectives. At specified intervals, typically monthly or quarterly, the board receives performance data and progress reports from the CEO and the key executive managers that allow it to keep a "balanced scorecard" of the organization's performance relative to business, mission outcomes, customer, member and constituent outcomes, and the internal working environment.

These balanced scorecard elements, frequently identified as "dashboard indicators," help the board maintain confidence in the enterprise and keep its eyes on the horizon rather than on the ground.

Program monitoring involves checking to see whether plans are being executed and desired outcomes being achieved. Program evaluation involves checking the quality of programs and services and determining whether the results are worth the funds and effort required. Boards concerned about some aspect of internal management or organizational performance customarily request an assessment by the CEO and, on occasion, an external review. Based upon the results of these assessments, the board may set new strategic, policy, or performance goals for the CEO and organization to meet. Certainly, if the organization experiences some crisis, the board may need to request more frequent updates and review more specific plans of executive management. Boards may even bring in an outside consultant whose objective view will help provide clarity. However, a well-run governance model as outlined here usually keeps organizations away from crisis.

The governing role requires executive leadership competencies. This does not mean board members must be experienced CEOs. It does mean board members must have demonstrated competencies in their work and professional endeavors and, when possible, their past governance service, relative to the crucial leadership requirements of the organization. While persons with professional backgrounds in law, finance, research, or fundraising might be tempting to put on a board, most of those specific technical capabilities can be found in staff, contractors, or consultants without wasting a valuable governing board seat simply to get "technical expertise." Governance is not so much about technical literacy related to a challenge facing the organization as it is about a broader peripheral vision of helping oversee a large, complex enterprise. **Think of governance as overseeing a forest rather than growing a single tree.**

Historically, many boards have typically made "technical" or "sector" appointments to compensate for a perceived lack of expertise in particular areas. Effective boards in the 21st Century are made up of individuals whose executive leadership competencies bring with them the ability to discern when to hire or contract for support in the technical aspects of their organization where they may lack hands on expertise.

When a board can find a member with leadership experience _and_ specific sector technical competence, it has achieved a valuable addition. Each board should be held accountable for defining the core executive leadership competencies desired for their governance model.

What are some typical executive leadership competencies needed of 21st Century governance?

- ~ Visioning and strategic thinking.
- ~ Organizational transformation.
- ~ Policy leadership.
- ~ Leadership succession.
- ~ Complex organizational enterprise acumen.
- ~ Innovation.
- ~ Governance roles and processes.
- ~ Self-awareness and integrity.
- ~ Interpersonal competence.

For other examples of leadership competencies see these resources (Leslie, 2009; OPM, 2013; Wallace, 2007).

Governance and Management Responsibilities Matrix

The governance and management responsibility matrix that follows (Table 2) contrasts the roles of boards (direction and oversight) and management (execution).

TABLE 2

Governance/Management Responsibilities Matrix

FUNCTIONS	GOVERNING RESPONSIBILITY	MANAGEMENT RESPONSIBILITY
Strategic Planning	■ Set mission and vision. ■ Determine organizational values. ■ Identify service philosophy. ■ Set strategic objectives (3–5 yrs.). ■ Ensure operational objectives support strategic objectives. ■ Approve major org. realignment. ■ Approve new services and expansion, cutbacks, partnering.	■ ID long-range operational and strategic issues for board. ■ Translate strategy into operation. ■ Implement change, monitor and report on progress. ■ Provide timely market data. ■ Act as a sentinel of business environment shifts. ■ Execute.
Finance and Budget	■ Establish annual budget. ■ Approve working capital and capital investment. ■ Approve variations from budget. ■ Ensure accounting system to track and monitor use of funds. ■ Support fundraising.	■ Conduct feasibility studies. ■ Financial forecasts. ■ Develop annual budget. ■ Prepare pro-forma budget statements. ■ Justify budget exceptions. ■ Manage cash flow. ■ Fundraising and capital development. ■ Investment analysis.
Operational Excellence	■ Ensure robust constituent feedback. ■ Ensure adequate quality processes: planning, evaluation, improvement. ■ Approve significant corrective actions and changes in service profiles. ■ Determine preferred organizational culture. ■ Regular review and update of policies.	■ Collect constituent input. ■ Routinely monitor quality indicators. ■ Special studies and corrective action as needed. ■ Review and update procedures. ■ Translate all board guidance into procedures and operations.
Audit and Enterprise Risk Management	■ Ensure regular financial and operational audits by external sources. ■ Establish "risk management" studies for vulnerable areas of operations.	■ Assure timely cooperation with external auditors. ■ Assist committee in identification of highly probable areas of organizational risk for annual study.
Public Policy	■ Develop strategic alliances and partnerships. ■ Maintain appropriate government, professional and org. relations.	■ Support professional activities. ■ Establish and maintain governmental, professional and org. relations. ■ Serve as communication link.

FUNCTIONS	GOVERNING RESPONSIBILITY	MANAGEMENT RESPONSIBILITY
Human Resources	■ Evaluate performance and set CEO objectives. ■ Approve org. salary and benefits. ■ Ensure legal and competitive human resources policies. ■ Ensure a leadership succession plan.	■ Recommend salary ranges. ■ Develop and manage HR system and records. ■ Performance management system. ■ Recruitment and retention.
Board Development and Succession	■ New member orientation. ■ Commit to in-service & conference attendance. ■ Succession planning for board. ■ Plan officer turnover. ■ Evaluate board performance. ■ Assess committee functions.	■ Assist new member orientation. ■ Encourage and arrange training. ■ Assist in identifying potential new board members. ■ Assist board evaluation process.

Board of Directors Legal Responsibilities

*"In their capacity as trustees, the members of the board of directors
must act at all times in the best interests of the corporation."*

Duty of Care

- Fiduciary Responsibilities: the responsibility board members have assumed to advance the organizational mission and oversee and protect its assets.

- Uphold the standard of "reasonableness and prudence." Regard and treat the organizational assets and other resources with the same care with which you would treat your own resources.

- Use your best informed judgment regarding what's best for the organization overall and periodically check the credentials and performance of those who serve the organization.

- Stay informed, engaged and attentive to governance work including a personal commitment to continued learning about the organization and high performance governance.

- Attend meetings, do your research, ask pertinent and challenging questions, raise ethical questions.

- Openly share your perspective regardless of majority or minority views of others.

- Use prudent judgment in the utilization of organizational resources including financial support for board activities.

Duty of Loyalty

- Disclose conflicts of interest immediately.

- Put aside narrow personal or professional interests to do what's best for the organization and all its constituents.

- Protect the confidentiality of sensitive issues and plans of the organization.

Duty of Obedience

- Support the organizational mission.

- Understand and obey the law, regulatory requirements and organizational by-laws, policies, values, and ethical standards.

Annual Duties of the Board of Directors

The role of the board of directors is to approve and monitor the strategic direction of the organization by creating financial plans, policies, and strategic plans that keep the organization successful.

The board hires one staff member, a CEO or Executive Director, to execute its strategy and policy direction.

Annual Duties:

1. Elect officers, appoint committee chairs and appoint new members.
2. Conduct external financial audit.
3. Review and affirm financial statement and IRS form 990 are accurate.
4. Re-validate and update the strategic plan.
5. Approve annual budget for the organization.
6. Evaluate the CEO and set annual goals, salary, benefits & bonuses.
7. Review by-laws every two to three years.
8. Check for needed policy updates.
9. Re-sign "conflict of interest" statement.
10. Conduct board self-assessment and set improvement goals.
11. Approve governance leadership succession plan and annual activity investment.
12. Nominate or select new board members for vacant positions.
    - *Many not-for-profits also expect board member annual financial contributions or fundraising.*
    - *Organizations with formal advocacy programs should annually review the performance of their lobbyist and the organization's advocacy plan and personnel.*

TABLE 3

Sample: Annual Board Decisions and Actions Calendar

Ongoing Governance	September	December	March	June
Finance	▪ Review year-end financials. ▪ Recommend annual budget. ▪ IRS form 990.	▪ Review committee charter and calendar.		
Audit / Enterprise Risk Management	▪ Review and approve audit plan. ▪ Recommend auditor for board selection. ▪ Internal auditor review. ▪ Internal auditor annual goals and risk assessment work plan.	▪ Audit results and management letter review. ▪ Review committee charter & calendar. ▪ Review ERM risk assessments and make recommendation.	▪ Review ERM risk assessments and make recommendations.	▪ Review ERM risk assessments and make recommendations.
Governance and Nominating	▪ Elections of new directors. ▪ Elect chairman and committee leadership. ▪ CEO evaluation begun. ▪ Maintenance of board calendar. ▪ Policy review.	▪ Conflict of interest policy signing. ▪ Policy review calendar established.	▪ Board self-evaluation. ▪ Discuss chair succession. ▪ Board leadership succession plan updated. ▪ Policy review.	▪ Committee chair succession. ▪ Committee chairs and assignments. ▪ Identify board nominations and new directors. ▪ Policy review.
Resources	▪ Discuss year-end solicitation plan. ▪ Develop and oversee solicitation of annual contributions.	▪ Review committee charter and calendar.	▪ Assess contribution levels per plan and make solicitation adjustments.	▪ Review resource development progress.
Board as a Whole	▪ Approve annual budget. ▪ Elect officers and new board members. ▪ Review IRS form 990.	▪ CEO evaluation. ▪ Act on committee charter reviews.	▪ Review board self-assessment and set goals. ▪ Review constituent feedback survey.	▪ Annual board strategic planning retreat.

Achieving a Policy Framework

*"A governing body should assure sound policy exists
for all critical areas of organizational risk and performance."*

The organization's major areas of risk and performance define where the governing body should ensure sound policy exists. The following are typical categories for policy development:

- Financial management.
- Strategic focus.
- Human resources.
- Management performance.
- Customer, member or constituent value.
- Governmental compliance.
- Ethical practices and behavior.
- Governance.
- Casualty /and loss coverage.
- Risk management.

All of these areas require appropriate structure and measures to assure organizational success. The governing body is responsible for setting the tone and architecture for how these functions and processes are fulfilled.

In simple terms, **a policy outlines the conditions within which the board expects these functions to be carried out.** Procedures, on the other hand, are internal guidelines for how polices and functions are to be executed. The board then holds management accountable for assuring that organizational processes, procedures, and decision-making fall within the parameters and spirit of its guidance.

In general a board should have a rolling two-year calendar of policy review. Begin with review of the highest risk policy areas to assure up-to-date relevancy and move through the rest over a twenty-four month period.

Achieving a Strategic Framework

"Strategy is about positioning the organization in an ever changing marketplace climate to remain viable, valuable and vibrant."

Changing Business Marketplace

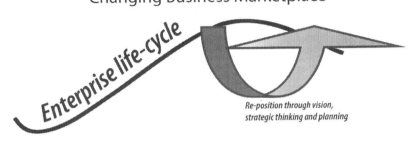

Re-position through vision,
strategic thinking and planning

Positioning an organization to remain vibrant is an ever changing and long-term challenge. High performance governance is aided greatly by a clear and current mission statement (Why do we exist?), an energizing vision statement (Where are we going?), and a clear statement of values (What are our standards for conduct?). Upon the sound basis of this framework, high performing boards conduct full strategic thinking and planning activities each year. This assures that the Board takes responsibility to check progress from the last plan and update assumptions, trend data, and objectives as necessary.

Further, boards should devote at least 50 percent of each and every meeting agenda to items directly relevant to the strategic plan. In the highest performing governing settings, upwards of 75 percent of the board agenda focuses on strategy: progress, re-calibration, trend discussions and continued focus on transformation toward the vision.

Applying Balanced Measures

"By keeping an eye on the critical dashboard indicators
of a 'balanced scorecard' the board maintains confidence
in the enterprise and is better able to keep its eyes
on the horizon rather than on the ground.

It's not uncommon for board meetings to stagnate into decimal point discussions of performance reports, departmental work plans, and second-guessing management decision-making. **The current operating norm for governance suggests that boards monitor organizational performance through the prism of a set of balanced measures. Balanced measures are 10 to 15 key measures that reflect performance on business results, customer service, product quality, and internal workplace environment.**

Maturing a balanced measures approach helps boards turn their oversight activity into the high-level policy and strategy work it should be: watching a set of dashboard indicators across the "balance" of the organization's work that indicates good health, caution or danger.

These measures, reviewed on a regular basis, give the board confidence that the parameters they have established (e.g. budget, customer satisfaction, staff retention, etc.) are being met. Typical indicators include:

TABLE 4

Business Performance	Customer Performance	Organizational Climate Employee Engagement
■ Budget performance. ■ Capital investment. ■ Operating reserve. ■ Sales and income. ■ Investments. ■ New business. ■ ROA/ROI/ROE. (Kaplan, 1996)	■ Customer value measures. ■ Customer satisfaction. ■ Complaints. ■ Repeat business. ■ Quality tracking. ■ Product and services performance measures. (Beckwith, 1997)	■ Employee climate survey. ■ Retention. ■ Employee and management development investment. ■ Talent succession. (Buckingham, 1999)

Many boards are now expanding the traditional dashboard with indicators that track board makeup and succession and economic or other indicators from their regional/national/global business environment.

TABLE 5

Board of Directors Dashboard	Environnment Economic Indicators
Board makeup profile to include: ■ Gender, diversity, professional background, competencies. ■ Age range <30, 30–50, 50>. ■ Board development to date. ■ Board members conference or workshop attendance; online training completed. ■ Number and names of potential board members in Leadership Succession Plan.	■ Federal interest rate. ■ Housing starts. ■ Unemployment. ■ Inflation rate. ■ International currency rates. ■ LIBOR. ■ Bond rates. ■ Other regional, national or international economic indicators relevant to your enterprise.

Distilling the traditional cattle call of numbers and progress reports from management into a balanced measures dashboard helps boards reduce unnecessary, dangerous, and time consuming micro-management behavior and reinvest their time in strategy.

Should any dashboard indicator become uncomfortably out of line, the board can then call for a more thorough assessment and report out by the CEO. Dashboard indicators are decided upon by the board to reflect the important facts of the business they consider relevant to track.

Reflection

Does your board have a clear set of key performance indicators across business, customer, member, constituent service and internal culture?

Where might board focus and efficiency be enhanced by development of a set of dashboard indicators?

Accepting Governance Accountability

*"Three components of governance accountability are particularly
critical to sustaining high impact governance: new member
orientation, leadership succession, and governance self-assessment."*

Just as the board holds the CEO accountable for the enterprise under the direction and parameters it sets, the board should also have a clear set of expectations and accountability for its own behavior. Board development, appropriate governance behavior, board leadership succession, individual member governance competence, committee work, and relationships with the CEO and management team, all require standards and regular evaluation. High performance boards conduct an annual self-assessment of their own functioning and set goals for improvement at that time.

Each board member bears responsibility for active participation in the governance process and support of the policy and strategy governance model. Specifically, each member is responsible for:

- Studying and understanding the organization and its business environment.
- Doing their homework prior to board or committee meetings.
- Actively participating in discussion and decision-making.
- Behaving as a supportive and respectful and appreciative team member.
- Protecting the integrity of the board and organization through ethical behavior.
- Strengthening their governance leadership competencies.

Officers have the added leadership responsibility of ensuring each member and the board as a whole meets governance expectations and stays on course.

Three components of governance accountability are particularly crucial to sustaining high impact governance:

- New board member orientation.
- Leadership succession.
- Governance self-assessment.

New Board Member Orientation

Assuming the board has a well-defined governance model and set of principles, new members need to be introduced to them right away and provided orientation to help understand them. Many boards make their governance model and board "job description" available to potential board members on their website. The information is useful to steer away those with inappropriate assumptions about serving on a board of directors and the time investment required. [See "Sample Board Orientation Scope" in the Support Materials section.]

Leadership Succession

The board is also accountable for leadership succession. It's not enough for the board to wait until a vacancy occurs to cultivate interest in serving or to begin developing governance leadership. For example, volunteer work that supports the organization and governance can provide a rich environment to educate and test commitment and leadership capabilities of potential board members. Inviting external "ad hoc" members to serve with board members on standing committees and task forces is another means of developing new leadership and finding fresh voices for board issues. Some boards have adopted an "associate director" category where next generation board members participate as a non-voting board member for a couple of years as a governance competency development strategy.

Leadership succession requires a robust plan supported by board commitment. It should be conducted with a systematic eye to the strategic issues of the organization and the ensuing board leadership challenges. Finding governance members who fit the life cycle and business environment of the enterprise requires due diligence, discretion and advanced planning. [See further specific suggestions in "Governance Leadership Succession and Recruitment" chapter .7]

Governance Self-assessment

"In a challenging economic environment with intense constituent activism and regulatory oversight, boards are working harder than ever to navigate uncertain territory and deliver on the promise of their mission. This may be a good time to step back and assess how your board stacks up to known elements of high performance governance."

Annual self-assessments are common practices among high-performing boards. Typically, a comprehensive assessment is conducted about once every three to four years. In the off years these boards assess a more focused area of governance such as meeting effectiveness, board development, strategic planning processes, or leadership succession. The best boards have a "Board Self Assessment Policy" to sustain future governance assessment (see samples in Support Materials Section). What might you wish to poll your board on this year to start a governance refresh?

Board Function

A starting point is to gauge perception of board performance on the major functions of governance: visioning, promoting the mission, strategic thinking and planning, and fiscal oversight. It's also helpful to assess the board's perception of its knowledge of programs and services and board/ management partnership. Surveying the board's confidence in how well it attends to each of these areas may expose opportunity for improvement previously unvoiced. Sample measurements might be: "The board makes timely strategic decisions in response to trends and changes in the business environment." "The board devotes sufficient time to strategic issues." "The board regularly reviews the spectrum of products and services to assure they support the mission and meet constituent value expectations." "The board ensures a climate of mutual trust and respect exists between the board and CEO."

Board Effectiveness

Perceptions of how well the board is structured, understands its roles and responsibilities and conducts its meetings offer valuable insight into the quiet concerns in board members' minds that frequently don't get entered into conversation. Additional questions around board makeup, leadership succession for officers and new board members and board development are also standard areas for governance assessment.

Sample questions might be: "Directors execute their duties consistently." "Directors have sufficient opportunity to express themselves on issues during board discussions." "Sufficient meeting time is allowed for true dialogue and reaching consensus on issues." "The current board contains a sufficient range of expertise and experience to be an effective governing body representative of our marketplace." "The board commits sufficient time to learning experiences designed to improve board effectiveness and understanding of high performance governance."

Targeted Issues

Self-assessments may also target specific programs or initiatives recently undertaken by the organization. Gathering the board's perception of the new marketing plan, virtual banking, CEO evaluation process, or specific committee performance allow customized feedback regarding high profile operations and processes. Surveys are not to get the board involved in management details but to gauge board confidence in how well the organization is delivering, thereby, opening valuable opportunity for strategic discussion or needed managerial updates.

Every Meeting Assessments

Conducting a short survey upon completion of each board meeting provides real time opportunity to stay on top of governance performance improvement and maintain a focus on high performance governance.

Try asking the following questions:

- Was the agenda appropriately prioritized based upon operational and strategic importance to our organization?
- Was there time for ample dialogue on each of our decisions?
- Were pre-meeting materials adequate and timely?

- Was sufficient time spent exploring strategic issues?
- Were all directors prepared and engaged?
- What adjustment would you suggest for future meeting efficiency and effectiveness?

Process

Paper or electronic surveys are commonplace. Numerous online tools such as "Survey Monkey" allow you to custom design your own survey. Many vendors and association management firms also offer proven self-assessment instruments.

Protecting each individual respondent's confidentiality is crucial to candid input. Standard survey technology suggests a 5-7 point satisfaction scale best differentiates agreement and finds central tendencies to perceptions. Typically a mid to lower satisfaction rating on a question prompts the respondent to provide further detail and suggestions thereby generating context to the rating.

Standard open-ended questions should include "What aspect of governance has worked particularly well the last couple of years?" "If the board could improve in only one area next year what would you suggest as a target?" "Any other comments or suggestions you feel might be helpful?"

You might also have your board consultant conduct a telephone survey every few years. Telephone interviews allow important follow-up questions, can discover latent tension and typically generate more suggestions than a less personal survey. I'm particularly fond of this modality because the interviewer has an opportunity to extract more context than most traditional paper or e-surveys. Typically each board member commits to a 45-60 minute phone interview around a set of questions agreed upon in advance with the board. In one recent survey I discovered much of the board felt dangerously dependent on the CEO. Fortunately the CEO sensed their lack of engagement and pressed for the assessment. The first assessment in 15 years with her board and a robust director development program ensued. On other surveys I've picked up concerns around board member public behavior, frustration with the secrecy of officer elections and CEO evaluation processes, and concerns with agenda management. In all these cases board members had been reluctant to confront the chair about their feelings and the assessment helped lead the board to a refreshed perspective on their work and effectiveness.

Suggestions for survey questions can be found in the Support Materials section.

TABLE 6

Board Self-Assessment Approaches

Type of Asessment	Approach	Implications
Real time each meeting.	Executive session upon completion of each meeting asks 3–5 key questions regarding governance meeting process.	■ Instant opportunity to surface issues and amend governance approaches. ■ Self-administered.
Annual focused assessment of one governance element.	Choose one element of governance to assess and improve (e.g. meetings, strategic planning process, CEO evaluation, committee functions, etc.).	■ Reduced burden yet fulfills a governance responsibility to self-assess governance processes. ■ Easily self-administered. ■ Effective for the 2–3 years self-assessment effort between full-spectrum governance assessments.
Full-spectrum governance assessment.	A comprehensive "soup to nuts" assessment of critical elements of governance conducted by an outside resource. Typical options: A. An assessment offered for sale by your professional association or governance vendor ($1,500–$3,000). B. A custom online survey (+/- $3,000). C. A custom telephone survey (+/- $3,000).	■ Common practice for boards about every 3–4 years or if significant change has occurred with organization, board membership, or processes. ■ Confidentiality critical, therefore, requires an outside resource.
Customized telephone survey.	Conducted by an external consultant (+/- $3,000).	■ These confidential interviews provide opportunity for more follow-up questions and specificity. Consultant can pick up on feelings an online survey cannot.
Board member to board member feedback.	Each member is asked to provide feedback to every other board member by answering the following question: *"What might name do as a board member to add even greater value to her / his governance contributions?"*	■ A more rare assessment modality yet gaining favor with some boards. ■ Requires a mature and engaged governing body. ■ If board is in extraordinary turmoil—an outside intervention is advised.

Reflection

How might your board begin a regular process of governance self-assessment?

A Board Culture of Governance Leadership

The board chairman of a not-for-profit international humanitarian enterprise recently asked me what a "culture of governance leadership" would look like. I've spoken and written quite a bit on governance, but have never quite framed my content in that context. It was an intriguing question and this chair was sincerely looking to move his board beyond simply being okay, to being great. Here are some of my thoughts.

Governance processes are how "culture" gets played out. Characteristics of 21st Century governance leadership includes:

- **A culture of open processes.** Most boards still work on an old model where a handful of senior board members and the CEO drive decision-making—not always in the open. A more effective governance culture is inclusive, open, and based on influence rather than being driven by a small band of cronies.

- **A culture of candid discussion.** A board that finds whispered hallway conversations going on because people don't speak their mind in a meeting is in for trouble. A culture of respect, encouraging differences of opinion, and providing ample time for discussion inspires ample dialogue so that all members may reflect fully on decisions is a healthier climate for leadership. Diversity of thought, necessary for innovative thinking and risk management, requires a safe environment for expression.

- **A culture of strategic focus.** A board culture of ongoing dialogue about the strategic future is more aligned with 21st Century challenges than one that spends time rooting around in mundane business matters. As suggested before, board meetings should be about 75 percent strategic and only 25 percent business oversight. The only exception is when the business is not doing well or the board is dissatisfied with CEO leadership.

- **A culture of absolute integrity.** Refusing to compromise integrity for selfish organizational or personal gain would have prevented the Enron collapse. Even though most boards have ethical decision-making, it's too precious a value to take for granted.

- **A culture of self-awareness and constant learning.** The most effective boards are constantly looking in the mirror at their own performance as diligently as they look at the CEO performance. Regular self-assessments, candid feedback to each board member about their contributions, and an unselfish board willing to replace themselves with members of a better fit, are some of the signs of this governance maturity.

Board culture gets defined by the values and behaviors of its members. Culture should always be relevant to the mission and goals of the enterprise. For instance, a humanitarian organization should have board members with both a passion <u>and</u> the competencies to lead within the scope of their mission. A board with an international scope of activities should have members who value diversity and who are competent dealing with the complexities of a globally diverse enterprise. A local board, such as a food bank or crisis center, should have a highly-defined sense of service, and competencies to tolerate difficult resource decisions posed by its constituents' needs.

Therefore, the board deliberately builds its culture with the values and behaviors of the new board members it selects. Which comes first, the selections or the culture? The answer is, culture may change as new sets of values and competencies are brought onto the board. For example, a board on which I serve is changing its culture as I write this. This change has come about because a few board members see the need to transform the board from a management culture toward a strategic governance leadership culture and have begun to promote new board members who represent movement toward that aim. With a tipping point of new and competent board leadership these members are now in a position to address their vision of culture more formally.

Leadership competencies are crucial to any governance leadership culture. The larger the organization and, or, the more critical its mission, the more critical executive leadership competencies are to its success—and to a governance leadership culture. Local boards frequently experience greater challenges in finding these competencies than boards that have drawing power due to prominence and size. Regardless of ease or availability, board chairs are responsible for making sure their boards have the defined set of core competencies they expect of governing leaders. "Professional backgrounds" are not core competencies. Surely an accountant is savvy in budget and finance but that doesn't make her strategic or service savvy. A contract lawyer, banker, human resources, philanthropy professional, or any other professional, does not necessarily have executive leadership competencies and should therefore, not be brought on the board simply because the enterprise has legal, financial or organizational problems—the board should hire staff and consultants for those tactical management objectives.

Some of the typical governance leadership competencies are drawn from executive leadership models (*not senior manager models*) and may include the following:

- **Visioning and strategic thinking**. The ability to see beyond the current organizational lifecycle by being aware of the shifting business horizon and thinking boldly about the next generation vision for the enterprise. Success can cause complacency. Complacency is why strategic thinkers are needed to challenge assumptions about the business model and the business environment.

- **Transformational leadership**. This is the ability to choose and support a CEO capable of organizational transformation toward a bold, strategic future. This also includes executive ability to create change sufficient to keep the organization vibrant and relevant without causing the enterprise to suffer. Transformation is fraught with chaos and tension which is why it is even more important to have governing members with transformational leadership experience and competence.

- **Governance literacy.** Governance work is much different from senior management or committee work and board members should have a firm grasp of the policy, strategy and leadership requirements of great governance. All boards are challenged with the member who wishes to dig into managerial operations. A culture of 21ˢᵗ Century governance leadership has members who hold the CEO responsible for managerial outcomes, and focus their attention instead on the policy and strategy direction necessary to maintain mission accomplishment.

- **Transparency.** An open and transparent decision style based on inclusive input and full board decision-making. The board member with this leadership competency will encourage participation with a mature sense of leading. They will bring awkward and difficult issues to the governing table, and work to assure that differences are dealt with in full light and not in backrooms.

- **Leadership succession**. A commitment to identifying and grooming the next generation of board members, including looking for the next generation of thinking that should replace yours. Exceptional boards work on creating a two-to-five year pipeline of potential new members.

- **Inherent Neurological Restlessness**. When boards become complacent with their success and stop looking for new models for their business they enter a period of slow death. Executive leadership competencies require board members who are comfortable challenging traditional assumptions about the business and looking for innovative models to best meet their mission.

Can a governance leadership culture that includes these competencies be sustained as board positions turn over? The answer is yes. Strategy, policy, goals, objectives, and personnel may all change but a culture of leadership can

be enduring. A legacy of exceptional board culture is sustainable if board officers demand this leadership culture, supported by contemporary leadership
competencies, and use it as a litmus test for new members.

Reflection

How does your board align with these characteristics of board culture?

Where might your board culture benefit from an open conversation and tune-up?

Creating a Legacy of 21st Century Governance

"As the science of leadership competencies overtook the art of leadership philosophies from the last century, new thought is being given to leadership at the governance level."

The pace of change in the business environment, coupled with the required transformation of organizational dynamics in the early decades of the 21st Century, is creating chaotic leadership challenges very different from the demands of former years.

Simply stated, organizational leadership behavior of the 20th Century was heroic and personality-driven. New research into the more complex environment of the 21st Century suggests leadership competencies are driven by transformation and sustainability. Now, competent leadership can be scientifically traced to behaviors less dependent on the CEO or board of directors as the source of all wisdom. Instead, successful organizations thrive on inclusive and transparent leadership involving customers and constituents. This new perspective on leadership is summarized in the graphics that follow.

Enterprise leadership focus has shifted in the last two decades as theory and competencies have moved from "heroic" to "transformational."

From Heroic	To Transformational
Independent	Interdependent
Dependent	Partnered and sustainable
Exclusive and closed	Inclusive and open
Push	Pull
Secretive	Transparent
Business results	Balanced measures
Limited input	Lots of input
Control	Facilitate

Stability	Change and transform
Operational	Strategic
Managed	Led

As the science of leadership competencies overtakes the art of leadership philosophies from the last century, new thought is being given to leadership at the governance level. Many organizational meltdowns of the late 20th and early 21st Century have been traced to old style boards conducting their governance with insularity and arrogance. As the lessons we've learned from Enron, WorldCom, Adelphia, and Global Crossing, for example, have unfolded, 21st Century governance oversight standards have shifted. So have the executive leadership competencies most critical to governance success. Governance in the 21st Century demands a higher degree of accountability, places greater value on strategic thinking and approaches business with much more inclusiveness and transparency. Summarized below are a few of the most recent shifts that might be cause for self-assessment and dialogue with your board.

Governance leadership shifts
from managerial oversight to
"strategy and policy" based governance

From Managerial Oversight	To Strategy / Policy Governance
Management decision review	Policy direction
Operational planning focus	Strategic thinking and planning
Protect status quo	Change and transformation
Exclusive decisions processes	Inclusive decision processes
Business results	Balanced measures
Constituent satisfaction	Constituent value
Behind closed doors	Transparent

62

CHAPTER 4

Board Agendas, Minutes, Committees and Task Forces

The effectiveness of governance work is highly influenced by attention to the "agenda" that guides board discussion and deliberation. Board effectiveness is also highly impacted by the work of committees and task forces who conduct detailed oversight and research and make recommendations to the full board of directors.

Frequent board review of these basic functions helps assure proper focus, effiency and positive impact. Possibly the following review of these functions will cause your board conversation to change.

Board Agendas and Meetings

Ninety percent of board members I talk with complain at some time or another about the quality of their board meetings. Too long, too short, not focused, too much detail, not enough dialogue, the list of complaints goes on. If you're reading this you're adding your own frustrating experiences. The "meeting" is where the legal work of the corporation gets done so regular assessments of meeting quality make sense.

Setting Agendas

The Executive Committee in consultation with the CEO sets the agenda and distributes it 7-10 days in advance of the meeting. It's the board's meeting, not the executive team's meeting. Assure the board drives the agenda. Traditionally a board agenda begins with approval of the previous minutes to assure an accurate legal record. Traditional agendas then typically consider "Old Business" followed by "New Business." **High performance agendas differ in that they place the most important items first and the less important items in descending order.** This has been the philosophy of effective meetings for decades but many boards still distribute critical items throughout and often find themselves rushed to judgment on key issues at the end of the meeting. "Prioritization" of items also should apply to committee reports: the most critical early, the least critical toward the end. In most cases committee reports can be included in the consent agenda if they have no action to recommend.

Agenda Mix

High performance boards spend about 25 percent of their meetings on fiduciary oversight (operational excellence) and 75 percent on strategy. Unless the enterprise is struggling, the future is your most important focus. The challenge is to streamline fiduciary oversight without unnecessary chitchat so the board can proceed to the transformational goals from the strategic plan. This is where "dashboards" of performance metrics and crisp reports of committee work contribute to efficiency.

Prioritizing the Agenda

Because financials are the foundation of fiduciary responsibility they should be an early agenda item for most boards. The items to follow should be prioritized based on the critical nature of the issue to the organization in either operational excellence or strategic movement. Every agenda item ought to be connected to one of those outcomes and the board, through the Executive Committee, should determine the order of importance. This month's merger discussion might come first while next month the strategic execution of a social media strategy might be first. The point is, priority occurs based upon the important contribution of decision making on that item to organizational success—both operational and strategic.

Consent Agendas

Consent agendas consist of a set of reports, updates, or routine actions (e.g., changing a signature for the corporation) that require no discussion. Typically the consent agenda groups items that really don't deserve discussion by the board. A CEO's report may go here even though there might be a "merger" agenda item later on for CEO update and discussion. Any specific item can be pulled for board discussion if desired. A committee report should go here if no board action is recommended. The critical point is the board can review these in advance, be fully up to date and save precious discussion time for more critical issues. I know from my own board service experience that if you give me a report as a formal agenda item I'm likely to talk about it even though no discussion is necessary. This behavior appears to be anthropological rather than diabolical.

Committee Reports and Actions

Committee recommendations to the board constitute formal agenda items. If the background report was in the consent agenda, all board members should be fully- informed and ready for dialogue and decision, thereby ready to move to motions and discussion right away rather than spending time on a drawn out history of the committee's deliberation. This is quite a challenge for many boards and where wasted effort frequently occurs.

Take the finance committee as an example. It is expected to have done detailed due diligence on financial reviews and other financial areas of risk. If there are no "exceptions" to report, the committee files its report, which is based on a dashboard summary of financial performance metrics agreed to by the board rather than multiple pages of financial data. The committee motions to accept the financial report as part of the minutes or note the exceptions in the record. The minutes capture any direction the board gives the CEO regarding the exceptions.

Other Agenda Presentations

No agenda item or presentation should be made to the board without advanced background information. Advanced information assures: (1) that we're fully prepared; (2) presenters don't waste our time with unnecessary background; (3) we have time for dialogue rather than death by Powerpoint™ presentation. This area is one where most boards can recover precious discussion time from overly verbal presenters. All presentations and recommendations from committees, the executive team or consultants should be presented in "executive summary" format, normally one page distilling the justification for the recommendation, with limited background notes, data or context. Well-done, executive summaries help boards move conversation to the critical issues rather than exploring trivial territory less relevant to the decision. [See more on "Executive Summaries" in the Support Materials Section.]

Board Minutes

Board minutes document governance attention to fiduciary responsibility for the legal corporation and provide a history of governance oversight. Minutes of committees and task forces are also part of the governance record of board due diligence in decision-making. In general, board minutes tell the story of deliberation, data review and actions taken. For legal purposes, if an action is not reported in the minutes it will be difficult for a board to later establish that it happened. Likewise, failure to record topics and issues of discussion and debate may make a board vulnerable to accusations that it failed its fiduciary duty of sound business judgments on behalf of the enterprise.

Boards will find wide-reaching guidance on how detailed minutes should be. The National Association of Corporate Directors ("Corporate Minutes" 2013), says, "Some groups emphasize 'short form' minutes that are little more than a detailed agenda while others recommend 'long form' minutes that are much more detailed". Simply understand that accurate and complete minutes provide evidence of a board's behavior. Many a legal battle has hinged on what was found or not found in corporate board minutes.

The National Association of Corporate Directors offers a simple framework of five elements to consider when compiling corporate minutes:

1. Clearly tell the story of actions taken: motions made and seconded, votes taken, and reference to the documents and materials presented and reviewed leading to the action taken.

2. Demonstrate director debate. The more important the discussion the more detailed treatment it should have in the record. High profile or high risk items (mergers, budget approvals, strategic plans) may take up more space than regular housekeeping items. Documenting materials reviewed by the board and questions raised can be done simply with a brief summary or more detailed narrative form based on a

board's desire. Certainly contrary opinions to any decision should be documented as part of the discussion that occurred.

3. Don't name names unless a director specifically asked to be identified. The minutes are a summary of the meeting discussion and documentation of actions taken not a transcript or "play by play" description of specific quotes or comments attributed to any one board member. This element has become more controversial for many boards whose members or shareholders are being more demanding in knowing who spoke to issues before the board, what they said, and how they eventually voted. Please check with your board attorney for guidance for your board here.

4. Demonstrate that risks were thoughtfully considered. As more boards are being challenged to attend to and document their approach to corporate risk taking, board minutes have become an essential means of demonstrating thoughtful and deliberate debate on risky issues. Minutes should identify the risks discussed by the board, the alternatives considered and contingency strategies discussed in case the decision or action later proved to be unsuccessful. In today's transparent and risk management environment "the absence of any of these types of discussions should be a red flag" (National Association of Corporate Directors, 2013).

5. Confirm accuracy and correct as necessary. Commonly, one of the first board actions at each meeting is to assure the prior minutes have been reviewed for accuracy and corrected as necessary. Directors should receive an advance copy of the minutes for study. Many boards have moved to receiving draft board minutes within 72 hours of a meeting. Whether this timing fits your needs or not, review and acceptance of the minutes as a legal corporate record is a board's responsibility.

As a legal officer of the board, the secretary is responsible for assuring accurate minutes are kept for meetings and retained in archives on behalf of the corporation. It's not uncommon for staff or another person to actually take notes that the secretary converts to legal minutes of the meetings.

Committee and task force minutes should be retained and this should also be an oversight duty of the secretary. These minutes further document full research and deliberation conducted on behalf of the board of directors.

Board Committees and Task Forces

"All committees and task forces should have a written 'charter'
outlining their purpose, makeup, boundaries,
deliverables and processes."

Board committee structure, as determined by bylaws, should support a policy and strategy focus. Traditional standing committees such as the executive, governance, finance, enterprise risk management and audit committee constitute the most basic needs of most boards. Committee functions do not diminish the authority of the full board; they simply provide a mechanism to divide work into manageable boxes.

Boards should create standing committees carefully. Standing committees should be reserved for the most basic and common of governance responsibility. It's much easier to appoint a task force than to disassemble a standing committee. Standing committees can take on a life of their own frequently annexing territory the board never intended for them to take.

Standing committees should be restricted to those that are required to attend to ongoing and sustained work facing the board. **In general, a shorter-term challenge should be given to a designated task force whose charter expires upon delivery of its product.** Frequently, having external "ad hoc" members serve with board members on these committees is a means of developing new leadership as well as ensuring fresh voices in board thinking.

All committees and task forces should have a written charter outlining their purpose, makeup, boundaries and processes (see samples in the Support Materials section). Remember, committees and task forces without written charters, accountable to the full board, frequently end up moving into territory they were never intended to explore.

Traditionally, boards would convene their officers (chair, vice-chair, treasurer, etc.) as an executive committee to design agendas and maintain oversight of all committees. In today's world more boards have created a "governance committee" whose charter it is to help assess board function, charge committees, review and update board policies, identify and develop potential new board members, recommend new board appointments and oversee board officer elections. As these functions have all become more critical and formal in contemporary governance practices they have evolved to a formal committee function.

Committee Charters

In support of the ongoing development and management of board activities, the **board executive or governance committee must assure clear and appropriate guidelines are provided for committee functions**.

Such guidelines, frequently referred to as charters, clearly distinguish the roles, responsibilities and functions of committees and their members, and are designed to clarify expectations and aid in board oversight. Each committee, subcommittee, task force, or ad hoc committee should have a written statement of charter.

Typical charters address:

Purpose

What outcome is the committee charged with producing? To make a recommendation? Only identify issues? Research, investigate? What's the deliverable? If it's changeable, re-clarify "outcome" expectations with each task order. Good charters begin with this fundamental clarity.

Timing

What are the milestones for performance reporting and completion? All committees should have an expiration or review date.

Authority

What is the committee authorized to do? Spend money, poll others, and represent the board? For example, Executive Committees may make decisions that are binding on the board.

Representation

What constituency does this group represent? A larger constituency than the board? If so, what's its obligation to them? To create product with this constituency in mind? Or, are they to create product with the interests of a broader constituency in mind?

Governance

How are decisions to be made? Is the process formal or informal? To whom does this group report? Who will chair the process? How is the chair decided? Are formal "Robert's Rules" utilized? How will proceeding records be kept?

Chairperson responsibilities

The chair is charged with calling meetings, setting the agenda, directing activities and assignments. The chair is also responsible for communication with the parent body.

Member responsibilities

Responsibilities are governed by charter and assigned by the chairperson. These may include specific committee functions such as meeting preparation, research, and communication. Fulfilling assignments and reasonable participation is important to maintaining a committee appointment.

Evaluation

What processes will the board use to evaluate the performance of the committee? How often will this happen. What "self-evaluation" is expected by the committee?

Annual report

Each standing committee should provide an annual report suggesting to the entire board the committee's next year's priorities.

Principles of Good Committee Work

Charters Required

All committees should have written charters clearly specifying roles, responsibilities, processes and deliverables. The simple description frequently included in corporate by-laws is usually not sufficiently specific to meet this need. Committees have been known to annex territory not originally intended by the board and a clearly acknowledged charter helps divert such messiness.

Commitment to Serve

Committee members should sign a commitment to serve, attesting they have read the charter and understand the time and responsibilities required of the appointment. This statement should also include a "conflict of interest" affirmation similar to what the board has signed. Having this sort of "service contract" in place always enhances the management of volunteers. A statement confirming that members serve at the will of board appointment provides the pathway for removal sometimes needed when committee members fail to meet expectations for effort or conduct.

Clear Outcome Expectations

While the charter spells out general responsibilities and processes, each deliverable charged to the committee should be explicitly articulated as an "outcome expectation." When we answer the question: "What would a good outcome look like?" we are more likely to provide the specificity that will assure quality, on-target committee outcomes. All tasked efforts should be clearly linked to either a strategic or operational goal.

Representation

Who does a committee member represent? This role definition question has become murkier as boards strive to assure diversity and inclusion in governance and committee participation. It is not uncommon for committee members to believe they represent a particular sector, constituency or membership characteristic and must act as the "voice" of that sector. Committee members most often are expected to represent the broad interests of the entire enterprise. If this is not the case then it should be clearly spelled out in the charter.

Transparency

Good governance is transparent to the constituency. Other than proprietary decisions or highly sensitive strategic work, committee work should be readily open for review by any constituent. Web site and e-bulletin board postings should assure access opportunity for those who wish to keep informed regarding the work of their organization. I like to see draft committee minutes available on the board web site within 72 hours of a committee meeting.

Inclusion

21ˢᵗ Century governance work is no longer the isolated activity of a select few. Good committee work is not limited to the intellectual capital of the board members but should also include substantial regularly refreshed constituent input. In the electronic communication era it is possible to get high volumes of input in short periods of time. Every constituent doesn't have to be polled. However, finding ways to check your progress, potential recommendations and the comprehensiveness of your issue review enhances all committee processes and should occur frequently. Contemporary "social networking" using an electronic focus group of sorts can leverage committee work from good to great.

Formal Pre-Announced Agenda

Surprisingly, this standard "rule of effective meetings" is overlooked frequently by committee process. Assure every meeting has an agenda, sent in advance of deliberation, with appropriate background information. While committee work may be a bit less formal than board meetings, structure still plays into effectiveness and member satisfaction.

Rules of Engagement

Committees are little spheres of teamwork being applied to organizational outcomes. Like any good team, committees need to have functional teamwork expectations that don't require Robert's Rules to manage. See "Board Rules of Engagement" as a starting point for this discussion with your committee teammates (Support Materials section).

Options

In some cases boards prefer a single recommendation from a committee. However, some committee outputs are best conveyed as a range of options, typically three, with each option making the case for its enterprise value. Single recommendations unnecessarily fence in board decision-making. Options give room for the final corporate decision to be more than yes or no. Sometimes, "both / and" is the right answer.

Creativity

Committees don't only exist to leverage the heavy workload of governance. Committees also assure broad intellectual capital weighs in on critical issues. For this reason, committees must work hard to assure fresh thinking enters their process. Many committees affirm the old saying that "a committee is a dark alley where good ideas are led to be strangled." A little creative abrasion, permission to think big, and a willingness to consider scary ideas is what keeps committees and organizations vibrant and valuable.

Reflection

How does your board committee performance align with high performance expectations?

Where might you begin refreshing structure and expectations?

When and How to use a Board Task Force

Board standing committees are established to perform the regular governance oversight and planning duties that demand more detailed attention such as finance, audit and enterprise risk management, government relations, governance, fundraising, etc.

Task forces are created "ad hoc" (temporary) to address a specific issue over a short period of time and then disband. For example, a board may wish a task force to explore a particular trend in their business environment and suggest positions, options or actions for board consideration. A board may need to assure inclusive input from key constituencies and use a task force to facilitate such input.

Questions to ask before creating a task force:

Is the organizational staff capable of answering the questions and identifying options?

- If Yes! Go to staff first. It's cheaper, faster, and affirms your staff.

- If No? Should you contract a subject matter expert or consultant to give direction to the board instead of using a task force?

- Do some of your constituents have the specialized subject matter expertise or diverse perspective you need for scoping a difficult and controversial issue? Ask them to serve on a task force for this purpose, thereby keeping the board's positions open until it's received the broader perspective.

Chartering a Task Force:

Providing a task force clear written direction and parameters helps assure success.

- Who is the chairperson and what are the responsibilities?

- What is the expected outcome? A recommendation? Options? Available literature or best practices identified? Be as specific as possible.
- What literature, constituents, best practices or other resources do you expect the task force to review/consider?
- How was the task force membership makeup determined and by whom?
- What resources or budget are committed to support the work of the task force?
- What limitations (parameters) does the task force have to work within: e.g. are they allowed to survey constituents on behalf of the board? Are they permitted to share records of their deliberations prior to their final product or recommendation? How transparent do you expect them to be in their work? Must they keep their work confidential to board only?
- Within what time frame is the task force expected to perform its responsibility? What's the due date for final outcome delivery? Are progress reports expected? What is the estimated time commitment for members of the task force? How is the deliverable expected? Verbal report, written report to the board?
- Is there a board liaison and what's its role?

Board Finance and Audit / Enterprise Risk Management Committees

Finance Committee

The traditional finance committee serves as the eyes and ears of the board on details of budget and overall financial affairs of the organization. Customarily, on a monthly basis, it convenes with the CFO to conduct a due diligence review of how the organization is performing on the approved budget and checks on reserves and investments. The finance committee also leads the board in setting the annual budget and creating a financial dashboard to carefully track the key financial performance indicators.

Since the Sarbanes-Oxley Act (2002) requiring corporations to conform to new standards in financial transactions and new IRS regulations for filing form 990, the role of board financial oversight has expanded significantly. New board committee structures typically include a separate audit committee that also includes "enterprise risk management" oversight.

Enter the Audit / ERM Committee

The 21st Century dawned like an angry hydra-headed monster attacking every known enterprise on the planet. In this environment the era of "Enterprise Risk Management" matured. ERM is business shorthand for the need to take a look at the full spectrum of risks associated with organizational leadership. ERM is quickly becoming the 21st Century equivalent of the quality improvement and customer focus movement of the late '80s. While much recent activity in financial services may be reactionary to the 2008 meltdown, ERM offers an important advancement in the way any business oversees its enterprise. ERM looks across the entire enterprise for risk and annually chooses non-financial risk areas for investigation. While adding more complexity to board responsibility, a separate Audit/ERM Committee deserves attention and movement.

ERM Dialogue

Before an Audit / ERM committee may foresee its ERM contribution, the board of directors needs to educate themselves about this approach. While the largest and most progressive organizations are beginning to hire ERM VPs, many organizations are slow to enter the dialogue. This becomes a strategic opportunity for board development. Devising a plan to understand the fundamentals of ERM, how ERM works in your business space, and what the implications may be for your organization is a worthy effort regardless of how far you take your formal execution of the ERM approach. This learning commitment may be a year long effort or more.

ERM Practices

ERM asks the organization to take a "corporate" view of risks. This involves a strategic look at risk across the business rather than within a series of silo views. ERM does not eliminate risk but rather provides a framework for the organization to identify and manage risks. **A risk is any event or activity that could prevent the organization from achieving its goals.** Typical ERM practice defines a several step process which can lead to avoiding, accepting, transferring or mitigating risks to the business. Many organizations already assess many of those risks in the financial arena by applying due diligence to Sarbanes-Oxley requirements. ERM expands the risk view spectrum to also look at such risks as business resumption plans, leadership succession, technology security, privacy, operational quality, insurance coverage, ethical behavior, performance management systems, personnel policies, and constituent complaints for example. The purpose of ERM planning is to anticipate risk areas and prioritize an annual plan for assessment and action. One organization's plan may be very different from another.

Risk Appetite

Boards should define the "risk appetite" for the organization. This appetite defines how much risk it is willing for the organization to absorb before taking action to reduce it. Risk appetite helps an organization balance the need for innovation with the threat of forthcoming damage.

Risk appetites may range from "adverse" to risk and active risk-avoidance mode to "open" to considering any and all risks. Many more innovative organizations fit the "risk hungry" appetite category because they are eager to be out ahead and willing to take the risks to gain potentially higher business rewards. One risk appetite may not drive the entire organization. It's possible different parts of the business may have different risk appetites that are quite acceptable to the board.

Today's boards, many in a more highly regulated environment than ever before, are finding the ERM conversation complex yet urgent. Board education in risk management should most likely be one of your top board development priorities. Board discussion of risk management should most likely be one of your top strategic initiatives.

Audit Committee

It stands as a natural evolution of the traditional finance committee function that a broader Audit/ERM footprint might be established as a separate entity. Certainly this puts pressure on several questions regarding the committee: Do we currently have the talent on the committee to address this broader risk function? Do we have size and resources to handle a full year ERM plan? What additional support should management provide and how affordable is it?

If your organization is large enough you probably want to look at converting a full time position to ERM leadership. If your board is typical, some talent upgrade may be involved as well as investment in committee development to fully comprehend the application of this new risk management approach.

Whatever your confidence with your risk management approach, convening dialogue around the ERM concept is educational and will most certainly lead to strategically different approaches down the road.

Reflection

What research and learning might the board undertake to assure it stays current with developing risk management practices in governance?

Is your organization large enough to warrant an internal auditor?
An ERM senior manager or vice president?

CHAPTER 5

CEO / Board Relationship

*The Board's responsibility is to help the
CEO be as successful as possible.*

Clear expectations form the basis for all good performance relationships. Therefore, the board must ensure the CEO clearly understands expectations for performance and interaction with the board. Certainly, timely communication as the year proceeds is critical, but so too are touch points for formal milestones. Formal, annual goal setting and feedback sessions, for example, should be supported by additional formal, semi-annual feedback. [See "CEO Evaluation Policy" in the Support Materials section.] The CEO feedback process belongs to the entire board and all should be involved; it is not solely a board president's or executive committee's responsibility.

Typical categories for goal setting and CEO feedback include:

- Enterprise operational management (e.g., financial, human capital, organizational climate, customer satisfaction, legal compliance, consultants).
- Relationship with board of directors (communication, responsiveness, integrity).
- Relationships with external constituents (e.g., government, accreditation, regulatory and oversight bodies, customers, funding sources, philanthropic sponsors, enterprise partners).
- Funding development.
- Strategic thinking.
- Ethics.

CEO Leadership Succession

Boards should expect the CEO to develop two succession plans: (1) Identification of who will take over in an acting capacity should the CEO not be available for duty; (2) a longer term development plan for higher level managers who may someday become CEO candidates.

CEO leadership succession, a critical commitment of any CEO and board of directors, suggests that a couple of high level managers of the organization ought to be identified as potential CEO successors. This doesn't mean they are ready now but that, with development, they have the potential to compete for the CEO job sometime in the near three-to-five year horizon.

Boards expect the CEO to identify these high potential leaders and provide coaching, mentoring and formal leadership development to guide their leadership maturation. Customarily, boards expect an annual report on this CEO leadership development initiative. Development of potential in-house talent does not mean a board is precluded from conducting a full external search should the CEO position become vacant. This should be public knowledge to all participants in a leadership succession program.

CEO Evaluation Process

Major contributors to a CEO's leadership success include:

- Competencies that match the leadership challenge:
    - ~ Does the board have clearly identified CEO leadership competencies?
    - ~ Does the CEO get the benefit of 360 Degree Leadership Feedback?
    - ~ Does the CEO have a non board member coach or mentor for support?
- Clear expectations for performance.
- Timely feedback.
- Annual goal setting.

A basic foundation for a successful board CEO evaluation process includes:

- An up-to-date CEO position description.
- Board policy for CEO annual evaluation and feedback.
- Board utilizing regular "executive sessions" to check perceptions on CEO performance.
- CEO performance objectives (goals) and measures set annually.
- Board clearly understands "governance vs management."
- Board conducts its own self-assessment annually.

The board evaluation responsibility encompasses contract, including salary, bonus and benefits; approving annual goals and work plans; providing timely mid-year feedback; and conducting a formal annual performance review.

A typical six-step evaluation process might look like the following:

1. CEO completes self-assessment for board. I recommend a personal, confidential 360-feedback survey to help the CEO self-assessment process.
2. Board surveys members for evaluative feedback and suggested goals, based on agreed-upon leadership competencies, past goals, developmental objectives, and data from customer and organizational climate surveys as available.
3. Executive or governance committee reviews input and creates draft evaluation and makes a salary and bonus recommendation. The governance committee might also conduct or contract a salary survey to guide this decision. Getting professional guidance is highly recommended in the current era of CEO compensation controversy.
4. Full board of directors reviews and approves evaluation, salary and bonus as appropriate.
5. Executive or governance committee holds feedback session with CEO.
6. Board finalizes evaluation, CEO goals, bonus, and salary increase.

Format for the evaluation feedback may vary but typical sections include:

- Performance relative to leadership competencies.
- Accomplishment on goals and objectives.
- Special accomplishments.
- Opportunities for improvement.
- Performance goals for the upcoming fiscal year.
- Rating:
  - ~ Needs improvement
  - ~ Consistently meets expectations
  - ~ Consistently exceeds expectations

This format might be graphically organized as follows:

Evaluation Criteria	CEO Self-Assessment	Board Rating	Notes
Leadership Competencies (50%) ~ Strategy ~ Transformation ~ Enterprise management ~ Customer focus ~ Board relations ~ Integrity/ Credibility			
Goal Achievement (40%) 1. 2. 3.			
Special Accomplishments (10%) 1. 2. 3.			
Leadership Development Goals 1. 2. 3.			

Board data for the CEO evaluation typically comes from these basic areas:

- Financial performance tracked at each meeting.
- Customer value and satisfaction data reviewed two times a year (surveys, focus groups, complaints).
- Organizational climate survey annual or as desired.
- Metrics around CEO goals for last year.
- CEO self-assessment.
- Board observations and perceptions of leadership competencies.

Typical CEO Leadership Competencies applied to the CEO evaluation and self-assessment include (but are not limited to): strategy development, transformational leadership, enterprise management, customer focus, board relations, integrity and credibility. These competencies are further delineated below.

Strategy Competencies:

- External awareness: trends, challenges, opportunities, threats, competition, governmental policy.
- Visioning: creating a common energizing vision.
- Strategic thinking: challenging traditional practices and seeing new models and partnerships.
- Strategic planning: seeing a roadmap for organizational transformation.

Evidence: clear future vision and game plan; staff clear on and supportive of vision & plan; strategic movement.

Transformation Competencies:

- Leading transitions and transformation.
- Systems re-design and re-engineering.
- Sponsoring continuous learning.
- Facilitating creativity and innovation.
- Developing and maintaining partnerships, coalitions, alliances and government relations.

Evidence: significant smooth change, strategic movement, new ideas, helpful partners.

Enterprise Management Competencies:

- Overall accountability and performance excellence in human resources, legal and other administrative duties.
- Financial management and budgetary performance.
- Engaged and involved organizational climate (annual employee engagement or climate survey recommended).
- Leadership succession development.
- Transparency.

Evidence: organizational efficiencies and effectiveness, transparency, engaged workforce, few organizational surprises.

Customer Focus Competencies:

- Creating and tracking value _and_ satisfaction.
- Services and products designed with customer input.
- Quality improvement efforts.

Evidence: customer surveys, voice of customer evident in changes and new offerings, quality review confirms quality and surfaces improvement opportunities.

Board Relations Competencies:

- Communication: timely, complete, transparent.
- Offers board options and alternatives.
- Supports and assists board succession planning.
- Facilitates board development choices.
- Meeting and agenda support.

Evidence: Full board assessment.

Integrity and Credibility Competencies and Personal Characteristics:

- Values and ethics beyond reproach.
- Continuous learning commitment.
- Political savvy.
- Personal and professional balance.

Evidence: constituents validate ethical leadership, continual learning results in improved leadership and new ideas brought to the board, obvious personal responsibility for mental and physical health.

CEO Goals

Every CEO evaluation should include specific goals for the coming year. What follows are sample goals.

Sample CEO Goal: Information Technology

CEO is charged with the assessment, research, and development of an organization-wide technology strategic plan for presentation at the June board meeting. Such a plan will likely address but not be limited to:

- Anticipated technology needs five years out.
- Current service assessment and risks.
- Proposed enhancements: hardware and software.
- Financial investment required: short and long term.
- Staffing implications.
- Return on investment.
- Potential support contractors.

Sample CEO Goal: Human Resources

CEO is charged with engaging a full scope organization-wide external review of human resources policies and practices (excluding compensation and retirement programs) for presentation at the March board meeting. Such an assessment will likely include but not be limited to:

- Policy and procedure review for completeness, organizational adherence and legal compliance.
- Hiring, on-boarding, performance management and termination, record keeping.
- Retention, turnover, career development.
- Leadership and management development and succession planning.
- Recommendations and suggested additions.

Reflection

Despite the board's confidence in your CEO evaluation and feedback process, what opportunities might exist to add even greater value to the process?

Have you re-engineered the CEO evaluation and feedback process within the last three years? If not, take a look. Even small adjustments can have powerful outcomes.

CEO Evaluation and Process Resources

360-degree feedback:

- **http://nefried.com/360/360goldshootout.html**
- **http://humanresources.about.com/od/360feedback/a/360feedback.htm**
- "Leadership Practices Inventory" **www.leadershipchallenge.com**
- Hay Group (**http://www.haygroup.com**) "Competency Portfolio 360 Assessment"

Leadership Competencies:

- Kouzes, Jim and Barry Posner. The Leadership Challenge Workbook (2012).
- Leslie, Jean. "What you need, and don't have, when it comes to leadership talent," Center for Creative Leadership (2009).
- Office of Personnel Management (USA). "OPM Leadership Competencies" (2013).
- Wallace, Les and Jim Trinka. A Legacy of 21ˢᵗ Century Leadership (2007).
- Zenger, Jack and Joseph Folkman. The Extraordinary Leader (2002).

Board CEO Evaluation Guidance:

- Kiel, Geoffrey, et. al. Board, Directors and CEO Evaluation (2005).
- BoardSource. Assessment of the Chief Executive Users Guide (2005).

Contracting:

- American Society of Association Executives (ASAEcenter.org) White papers "Compare and Contract" and "What to Watch for with CEO Contracts."

CHAPTER 6

Strategy and Strategic Thinking

"Evolution keeps you alive.
Revolution keeps you relevant."
Gary Hamel, <u>Leading the Revolution</u>

Organizations exist in a live business environment where elements of economics, customer value, technology, social and political shifts and leadership competencies and expectations are constantly changing. These ongoing changes mean that static organizations, those that do not adapt, will lose relevance.

Strategy is about positioning the organization in the marketplace to remain viable, valuable, and vibrant. Positioning is an ever-changing and long-term challenge. Frequently, an organization's biggest competitor is its own provincial view of its future. To remain relevant, organizations must admit the need to change or migrate to new positions within the business marketplace. Progressive organizations do this by capturing developing opportunities, neutralizing threats, leveraging strengths and strengthening weaknesses. The strategic plan becomes the organizational road map for future success.

High-performance organizations also regularly engage in **strategic thinking** exercises and at least annually conduct a strategic planning event. High performance boards of directors assure that at least 50 to75 percent of each board meeting agenda focuses on the strategic plan for: progress, problems, validity, and business environment shifts. Board members should be involved upstream in strategy development rather than downstream after staff, committee or consultants have drafted a plan.

Re-position through Visioning, Strategic Thinking, and Planning

Vision is the component of strategy that defines the desired position of the organization within the shifting business environment. Vision should be a common, energizing view of what the organization intends to become. Migration toward the vision brings the organization closer to a viable and valuable business position- characteristically focused on a 3-to-10-year horizon.

Strategic thinking answers the question: "How might we re-design our enterprise to leverage leading edge marketplace and business models?" Strategic thinking requires bold thought about what the organization can become and how it might dynamically be transformed in the business environment. Strategic thinking challenges assumptions and traditional boundaries and partnerships, and anticipates new models.

Boards should think of strategy development as more of a process than an exercise to be completed at a retreat. High performance boards are engaged in strategy development and re-calibration at every board meeting. They use the annual retreat to further explore complex elements of their business environment and their offering and "pressure test" their strategy (Bradley, 2011).

Strategic Thinking

"Professionals generally know so much about what they know that they are frequently the last to see the future differently." Edie Weiner & Arnold Brown, <u>Future Think</u>

TABLE 7

PLANNING	STRATEGIC PLANNING	STRATEGIC THINKING
Key Question: "Are organizational activities goal-directed, organized and monitored?"	**Key Question:** "What is our desired business position and how must we change to assure its accomplishment?"	**Key Question:** "How might we redesign and transform our business to leverage leading-edge business models?"
Management Activities	**Leadership Activities**	**Innovative and Visionary Activities**
■ Policy and financial oversight. ■ Evaluating inefficiencies. ■ Identifying improvement objectives. ■ Outlining action steps. ■ Establishing control systems. ■ Twelve month cycle view. ■ Celebrating achievement. ■ **Execution.**	■ Identifying an alternative future position. ■ Anticipating opportunity and threat scenarios. ■ Setting organizational change priorities. ■ Designing change pathways and strategies. ■ Evolving and adapting systems. ■ Outlining change in formal plans. ■ Three to five year cycle. ■ Course corrections regularly. ■ **Change.**	■ Challenging core business assumptions. ■ Confirming stakeholder value shifts. ■ Anticipating and projecting lifecycles of products and services. ■ Re-inventing the business. ■ Strategically explore innovation of others in your business. ■ Sponsoring paradigm shifts and pilot tests. ■ Stretching—merging boundaries and partnering. ■ Bold innovative movement and sweeping changes. ■ **Transformation.**

Values Are Migrating: Is Your Organization Moving with Them?

In his watershed 1996 book on value migration, Adrian Slywotzky suggested organizations wake up to the speed with which customer (also read member or constituent) value was shifting (Slywotzky, 1996). He reminded us all to keep a close eye on the stages of our product and services lifecycles and be watching customer shifts more closely.

Slywotzky's call for increased awareness and less complacency came before it all started speeding up for real. Google beta launched in 1998, the iPod and Wikipedia showed up in 2001, and Web 2.0 was declared by 2004. Recessions hit the European Union again (2000-2001) and the world changed drastically with the 9/11/2001 terrorist attack on the United States. World economies have faltered ever since with U.S. corporate failures in 2008 and the most recent European Union financial crisis. Now we see a new cycle of unrest in most of the Arab world.

As the Millennium dawned talk turned to the aging population, the value shifts of Millennials and how technology was accelerating differences in generational behavior. The 24/7 instant news cycle, bloggers turning over rocks everywhere, social media exploding, and desktop computers left behind for tablets and handheld devices have forever changed access to information.

Value migration (evolutionary shifts in values) has given way to volatile value bounces where shifting trends accelerate at such a velocity they seem to skip a step. It was only three years ago I heard a financial institution CEO tell its chief marketing officer not to bring up mobile banking again. It was only a few years ago that professional associations could count on the next generation of members to sign up automatically. It was only a few years ago that the millennial generation was badmouthed as lazy and selfish only to discover today they are volunteering and philanthropic in a ratio to their wealth similar to that of baby boomers.

In today's world the VUCA (Volatile, Unpredictable, Complex, Ambiguous) principle, first articulated by the Army War College, rules our business environment (Johansen, 2007) and challenges us all to stay alert to changing expectations. What does this unpredictable acceleration in value

101

shifts have to do with how you must lead your organization? You might wish to take several immediate gut checks in the following areas:

Metrics

How well are you tracking customer, member and constituent value? Value is different than satisfaction. Value refers to the benefit accrued to the person who does business with you. Ask your hometown hardware store—if you can find one--what big box price and selection has done to their business. Today's organization should be formally tracking customer values with quarterly surveys and daily "real time" web connections such as blogs, Facebook, and Twitter. The once a year "check-in" on how our customers are feeling and thinking has gone the way of vinyl records. Can you compare today's survey of customer wants, expressed needs and wishes with three years ago? A year ago? If so, you can see emerging value shifts early and begin redesigning your products and services today.

Benchmarking

Out there somewhere are organizations way ahead of you in product and service innovation. These risk takers see trends over the horizon and like to be first to the next future. Frequently they can afford to launch early and are talented enough to re-design in fast moving space as feedback comes in and hiccups are identified. Who are these folks in your industry? What are they doing that seems so scary you think they might be crazy? By tracking three to five of these organizations and their portfolio of changes you can energize your strategic planning process, stretch your own thinking, and discover new questions you should be asking your own constituency about the next generation of services and products.

Engage employees

Ever wonder what your employees are thinking today? If you're relying on the once-a-year employee survey to find out, you're getting out of date quickly. The employees are talking about your organization right now. Technology makes this possible without management's permission. Find out where they talk about your organization and its culture and listen in. Better yet, give them a virtual outlet within your organization so you're a partner in the conversation rather then a limp listener. You'll be surprised how quickly you can get a feel for climate change in your culture. Wherever you need to go in the future and however fast you need to move you'll need highly engaged employees moving right along with you.

Innovation

Internal to your own organization are hundreds of new ideas-—ideas for refreshing your current portfolio, bringing in new thinking, and even designing "new, new" designs. To get a feel for how fast innovation is moving as a "core competency" of organizations read *Fast Company* magazine regularly. Put together a virtual focus group of big thinkers and critics within your own organization and use them as a think tank of possibilities. If you can't handle the chaos and criticisms that come from that you might not be ready to keep up with the future.

Crowdsource your customers, members and constituents

Somewhere in your universe of constituents, new thinking is evolving about your value to them. Why not give them a microphone and listen carefully to the conversation? Social technology, not to be confused with social media (Hearst, 2009), provides ample opportunity to invite constituents into the design laboratory. Find a cadre of your most vocal, possibly even more critical members or customers and crowdsource their thinking on a regular basis (*DailyCrowdsource*). If you serve a population with less access to technology, pull together small face-to-face focus groups and explore their voice about your product and services.

Biggest critics

What are your biggest critics saying about your organization, your portfolio of offerings, and your methods of operation? Don't dismiss them, embrace them—there's gold in their observations. While the disgruntled frequently don't apply the same political savvy or manners of other customers, members or constituents they do represent a set of eyes and ears that might signal future value shifts. Recent movement in "transparency," "customer/user blogs," "real time information," "product enhancements," "customer/member choice," "virtual education," all came about because disgruntled constituents pushed organizations to keep up with shifting values and available technology.

Strategy Implications

for the Viable, Valuable and Vibrant Organization

*"A strategic plan should energize the organization
around its possible future."*

It wasn't too many years ago that one could still find organizations without a strategic plan. I ran into one just last year. However, in today's business environment it's rare to find an organization of any type, for-profit or nonprofit, without a strategic plan.

The importance of an organizational strategic plan has drawn consulting enterprise into the planning marketplace with enough options, approaches and models to make your head swim. You can still "SWOT," or even "SOAR," "Scenario," and certainly "Aspire," your way to a plan for alternative futures (Starvos, 2009; Ioannou, 2012; Wade, 2012). According to Wikipedia, a determined organization can also "PEST," "STEER," "ATM," and "EPISTEL" its way to the future.

Strategy is an integrated set of actions designed to create a sustainable vibrancy to your mission or an advantage over your competitors. For many organizations, strategy is opportunistic and reactive when the business environment pressures the enterprise. For successful organizations, strategy is proactive and about constantly migrating to a new position in the business environment. For high performance organizations, strategy is about brainstorming and creating new entrepreneurial and innovative approaches to stay ahead of a rapidly changing business environment.

Strategic Thinking

Creative, entrepreneurial insight into a company, its industry, and its environment by challenging assumptions, value tracking constituents, and looking at the lifecycles of products and services.

Formal Strategic Planning

Systematic, comprehensive approaches to developing strategies for continued migration to adapt or stay ahead of business environment changes.

Opportunistic Strategic Decision Making

Effective responses to unexpected opportunities and problems—more reactive than proactive.

Whatever your approach, the board and executive team need to understand exactly why they need a strategic plan and agree upon a methodology to jointly develop and maintain a strategic focus. The "why" is easy: a rapidly changing business environment threatens a complacent organization yet provides success opportunities for the alert organization.

Developing a plan typically means the executive team leads the board in a scan of the business environment, and an honest assessment of the organization and its talents and competencies. This scan should digest customer, member, constituent, and competitor data. This process results in the board and executive team jointly setting goals for assuring future success. A strategic plan should give confidence that the organization can be viable (alive), valuable (relevant to a constituency) and vibrant (dynamic). A strategic plan should energize the organization around its possible future.

Despite the abundance of planning approaches the most common question I get is "what are the typical domains covered by a strategic plan?" Drawing upon 30 years helping organizations think in the future tense, I'll be bold enough to summarize these typical domains below. This doesn't mean your plan needs to look like this—it's only an anthropological summary based upon my experience. It's not uncommon to find the following areas where organizations have live strategic objectives:

- Operational Excellence.
- Sound Financial Management.
- Technology Solutions and Accelerators.
- Customer, Member, Constituent Engagement.
- Branding.
- Advocacy / Regulatory.
- Governance Leadership.
- Philanthropy.

Let's take each domain and outline what I often find organizations attending to as strategy.

Sound Operations

Certainly as technology, competitors and customer demands shift, it's necessary for operations to also adapt. Most organizations that put "operational" goals in a strategic plan do so because they have fallen behind and need to elevate the importance of improvement. Typically, when operational matters are in sync and performing well, they drop off a "strategy" dashboard and onto the management team's "operational" dashboard.

Common areas for attention are leadership and management excellence, organizational structure, organizational culture, automation, innovation, workforce development, lean process and quality improvement, and customer focus. In many smaller associations it may be enhancing the service from the contract management company.

Sound Financial Management

In a strong economy it's unusual to see financial management goals in a strategic plan. 2008 was a wake up call for every organization on the planet, however. Boards and management teams have been forced to take a fresh look at economic downturn, customer demand, and financial strength to sustain the organization. Cutbacks, layoffs and delayed purchases were all executed to skinny down expense, protect capital needs, and live for recovery.

2008 changed the conversation in every boardroom I know. It's now common to find boards weighing in on the strategic plans to keep the organization well capitalized, protecting reserves for a rainier day, and closely examining margins and products to assure focus. In the financial services industry, stretch goals for financial performance are commonly found in the strategic plan.

Many boards are also including improvement goals for their finance and audit committees. As financial oversight grows more complicated, selecting and developing committee and board members around fiscal literacy is crucial. In corporate America, 47 percent of finance committees are chaired by a board member who is or has been Chief Financial Officer (NACD, 2013). Audit committees are increasingly taking on broader Enterprise Risk Management (ERM) and it's quite common for focus in the ERM domain to make it into the strategic plan.

Technology Solutions and Accelerators

Technology in general, and social technology more recently, has always been cause for strategic planning focus. Information technology hardware and software capability have typically shifted so quickly (quarterly most experts say) one must stay strategic to keep up. How recently has your organization undergone a "core conversion"? How recently have you "shock tested" your information technology security? How well do technology applications drive your customer relationship management and cross-selling initiatives?

The more recent growth of a networked globe has changed how organizations engage their employees, customers, vendors, contractors, funders, regulatory officials, competitors, and the media (Hearst, 2009). Networked social technology is no longer peripheral to any organization; it is core to the future.

Information "technology capacity" and "social technology" strategy are here to stay in our strategic plans. Many experts believe they should be separate domains of a strategy, each with its own challenges, philosophies and goals. I agree. In the 21st Century I urge every organization to have both domains separate and accounted for in their strategic plan.

Customer, Member, Constituent Engagement

As the 21st Century dawned, customer pressure and selectivity increased while choice exploded. These forces forever changed the old 1990s conversations about "service." Service is now too abstract a concept for strategy. Instead, the new "customer experience" approach encompasses customized products and channels, customer input into design and pricing, web-based showrooms, virtual intelligence, communities of users and purchasers, speed, organizational accountability and full transparency. "Big Data" now dominates how organizations must sort through customer expectations, and satisfaction is now paired with "value" as common research interests (McAfee, 2012).

Customer data must now be crunched with geometrically more combinations than 10 years ago. Woe to the organization that can't articulate the customer value proposition and how it's changing. Many boards are expecting to see data in this strategic arena at least quarterly.

Satisfaction is now a complex set of questions about the "customer experience" and value is now prone to mass customization. Boards must set rising expectations for organizational performance and continuously refresh strategy. A strategic plan without goals and expectations for adding great customer value is inadequate.

Strategic planning and member choice has grown in importance for associations. A one-size membership category no longer fits and members are now expecting to choose between whether they wish to receive the newsletter or journal, even whether they wish hardcopy or e-versions. They also expect to pay differently for their choices. The most recently-published works on associations indicates major member engagement change is in play—your association should have something in its strategic objectives about how you plan to adapt to the generation of new expectations (Coerver, 2011; Sladek, 2011; Gammel, 2011).

Branding

Brand and brand management is showing up more commonly in organizational strategic planning (Ries, 2002; Beckwith, 2012; Aaker, 2011). Branding is a way of organizing the institution's strategies to present a consistent and well thought out impression to customers. It involves identifying and highlighting the attributes that differentiate the institution from its competitors, infusing that message into everything it does, creating or updating services to support the brand and measuring results.

Brand goals are frequently a subset of the customer focus goals. However, the rapidly-shifting customer and competitor landscape elevates branding to its own strategic domain for many organizations. If your organization confuses its branding with its marketing campaign then maybe a tutorial at your next board meeting would be useful.

Branding strategy makes sense if your organization finds its customer, member, or constituent base shifting, competitors taking away market share, or customers questioning your value or credibility in a new economy. Re-branding is a frequent strategy in today's global economy. Branding refresh—using different or newer mechanisms to define who you are—is now common and most likely necessary every few years.

Advocacy and Regulatory Response

Associations are typically involved in advocacy for their profession or business domain. Everyone is involved in adapting to shifts in regulatory oversight. For associations, advocacy goals are consistently represented in strategic plans, most commonly because the economy, government oversight, credentialing, hiring practices and overall professional or business value are always being challenged.

For groups in healthcare and financial services, regulatory chaos has been in play for several years and is not likely to settle down in the next few years.

Therefore, refreshing your strategic goals for influencing external oversight as well as new adaptive strategies to shifting regulations is crucial. While many larger organizations have seasoned government relations staff, it is still critical for the board to recognize and focus strategy in its strategic plan. For smaller organizations, it's even more crucial, because the executive team and board are playing the major influence and education roles as part of the advocacy agenda.

Governance Leadership

Since the Sarbanes-Oxley act (2002) in response to corporate accounting scandals of Enron, Tyco and others, the conversation has changed in every boardroom about accountability, fiduciary oversight, and the required talent for a competent board of directors. A 2012 BoardSource survey reveals at least 40 percent of board members admitted they didn't fully understand what they are supposed to do (Boardsource, 2012).

In the last 10 years about 75 percent of the boards I've worked with have invested some element of strategy in governance leadership. At the basic levels, developing greater board governance literacy is a common strategic objective. More complex strategic goals frequently surface around board leadership succession and board ERM responsibilities. Boards that conduct regular self-assessments will always find some element of governance needing attention—frequently it's significant enough to surface as a strategic goal. Another reason for elevating governance leadership goals to the strategic plan is to make them visible to regulators and outside constituents who appreciate seeing how the organization recognizes governance's critical role in business success.

Philanthropy

Non-profit boards in general, and particularly those in the domain of cause-related fundraising, will have goals around philanthropy. As the landscape of causes and organizations seeking funds has exploded in the last decade, more and more boards invest substantial strategic dialogue in developing goals that keep up with competition and donor behaviors. As traditional means of fundraising, such as galas and walks come under greater stress, more and more boards are moving to social networks, on-line campaigns and targeted spokespersons to maintain their philanthropic funding pipeline. For example, two of the most recognized and respected cause fundraisers, the American Heart Association and the American Cancer Association, have recently gone through a major refresh in their on-the-ground approaches to local governance and engagement. When the big girls and boys recognize a changing and more challenging philanthropic marketplace, it's time smaller players also wake up.

Because boards are so crucial to philanthropic fundraising success, it doesn't matter if they have high powered experts on staff or not—the board must get in this game—and articulating strategic goals is a means of doing so.

What About Your Strategic Plan?

If strategic goals aren't stretching your organization to change, you don't have a strategy. Instead, you have a reactionary plan to stay afloat and are most likely only reacting as changing conditions hammer you.

As explained above, not every organization will have all of the strategic domains discussed here in its plans. However, it would be challenging to find any strategic plan that couldn't be easily nestled within these domains.

Finally, I've seen many a great "paper strategic plan" of numerous goals and tactics with pages of accountability. While good for your consultant's ego, many of these are too complicated for the average organization to manage. The challenge is to decipher the changing landscape and focus on the vital few strategic priorities that will transport you to your desired new future. These are usually three-to-five, or at most, five-to-seven strategic goals. More goals than that and boards and management teams tend to get distracted, and something falls off the plate. What are your vital few? Take a few moments at the next board meeting and scan your plan to identify the top three strategic goals where success is most crucial to your future. Then, discuss and check in on those goals at every meeting!

Reflection

Does your board "refresh" your strategic plan each year?

If your organization could only focus attention on two of your strategic goals which ones would be critical to accelerate organizational accomplishment?

Future Proofing Your Board of Directors

"Nothing ages faster than the future."

The future is aging faster and faster, tossing us new wild cards every day. Many experts are deeming this chaos the "new normal." Assuming reasonable operational and financial health of your organization, in the new normal, your most important governance contributions are positioning and repositioning the enterprise and your board. The early 21ˢᵗ Century taught us that while we can't always predict the future, having a future tense-focused board of directors reduces surprise, enables nimbleness in response to sudden change, and seizes opportunities ahead of the average organization.

Remember "VUCA"? If you're on a board of directors or involved with governance issues as a professional, you're living an environment that's replete with Volatility, Uncertainty, Complexity and Ambiguity. Welcome to the 21ˢᵗ Century—or what mega investor Warren Buffet calls the "new normal" for business and enterprise of all types.

In this environment can we really "future proof" our enterprise from volatility and chaos? Proof, no; prepare to be less surprised, react earlier, and be nimble with counter movers…yes! What follows are a few tactical investments to gain greater future tense sensibility. While we can't predict the future we can certainly anticipate it. Think in general about investing heavily in the following behaviors:

- "Sentinel" watches on key indicators and trends in your business.
- "Discourse" on these trends and indicators—real dialogue and exploration not simply reporting out and moving on.
- "Scenario thinking" with "what if" questions and exercises designed to create alternative desired futures as possible reactions if trends move up, down, faster, slower, or peter out.
- "Course corrections" quickly. If your board and executive team have created a pipeline of futures exploration and discussion as discussed below then knowing when and how to re-calibrate plans is easier and

keeps you from knee jerk responses every time an indicator shifts in your environment.

Adaptation and ultimately transformation of your enterprise to a shifting environment are primary responsibilities of governance. Invest in these tactics to assure fidelity to that responsibility.

1. Spend 50 to 75 percent of each board meeting on strategy: review and update a strategic objective, discuss a significant trend—bring a strategically relevant article, book, or data to look over.

2. Explore issues and opportunities at your annual retreat with paradigm shifting questions: "If money were no object what would we do?" "What would our younger customers, members or constituents like us to do?" "If we had to merge or partner with someone to stay in business who might that be?" "If we could only accomplish one or two strategic initiatives this year, what should they be?"

3. At your strategic planning retreat begin with "strategic thinking:" challenging assumptions about your current models, looking for innovation across other organizations and industry domains, talking about some of the highest risk innovation going on in your industry.

4. Bring an outside trend expert in your domain to speak at your annual strategic planning meeting to stretch your thinking about the future. Bring in two to three during the year to speak to your board.

5. Explore your value proposition to constituents by doing a deep dive into your customers', members' or constituents' answers to a twice-a-year "value" survey. Satisfaction is how happy they are with service and access; "Value" is what needs customers want you to meet and how their needs are changing.

6. Expect executive and key administrative staff to push new developments your way on a board only web site—especially have them report

on trends they noticed while attending professional meetings. Give your CEO and executive team permission to scare you with big ideas.

7. Target a specific topic or issue for investigation when you go to an industry meeting and network with those who are making innovative moves to pick their brain. Report back at the next board meeting or invite your new contact to your board meeting to share the experience.

8. Attend professional meetings outside your industry on topics pertaining to your interest in future trends, such as leadership succession, technology, mergers, government regulation, innovations, or social media.

9. Put together a "think tank" of advisors with whom you meet twice a year to discuss the future of business in your domain. No, those casual chats with peers at the regional meetings don't cut it—get a diverse group of thought leaders and have them think out loud about the developing future they see.

10. Provide books, journal and magazine subscriptions for your board as a means of stretching their thinking about the future. Some suggestions: FastCompany magazine; The Futurist (World Future Society); The Economist magazine; Out of the Blue: Wild Cards and Other Big Future Surprises (John Petersen); Blue Ocean Strategy (W. Chan Kim); Peripheral Vision: Detecting the Weak Signals that Will Make or Break Your Company (George Day); The Extreme Future, James Canton; The Meaning of the 21ˢᵗ Century, James Martin.

"To be responsible inventors and discoverers, we need the courage to let go of the old world, to relinquish most of what we have cherished, to abandon our interpretations about what does and does not work." Margaret Wheatly (2006)

Essential Components Of a Working Strategic Plan

"Strategy is about positioning...positioning your enterprise within a changing business environment to remain viable, valuable, and vibrant."

1. **Envision your enterprise three to five years out.**
    *   Be Bold. Dream. Be specific.
    *   Describe this future in as many ways as you can possibly imagine.
    *   Imagine business mix, areas of growth, financial situation, new markets or products?

2. **Envision your organization when you have arrived at your three-to-five-year vision and work back from there.**
    How did you get there?
    *   Of what opportunities did you take advantage?
    *   Were there threats or weaknesses you neutralized or overcame?
    *   What significant changes did you make?
    *   Any revolutionary initiatives?
    *   Risks you took?
    *   Partners and others who helped you?
    You have just created a high-level summary of your possible game plan.

3. **Convert your vision and your potential game plan into the five to seven most vital few (highest impact) strategic objectives.**
    An objective is simply an outcome you wish to achieve. Five to seven of these ought to align with the vision you laid out in step one.

4. **Identify the research or creative thinking necessary to validate your vision, strategic objectives and potential tactics for these vital few objectives.**
    *   What data might you need to confirm your assumptions?
    *   Are there existing benchmark organizations? Who are they?

117

- With whom might you partner or collaborate to achieve your goals?
- Who might be able to give you a good "sanity check" on your plan?

5. **For each strategic goal, outline...**
   - Tactics and actions.
   - Milestones (quarterly usually works).
   - Resources (who, budget).
   - Measures of achievement.
   - Revisit this tactical plan at least once a quarter.

Constructing a Strategic Plan: Some Typical Basics

**Ask yourself these questions and sort out the data
as suggested below.**

- **What's been accomplished in the last 24 months?**
  - ~ It's always nice to build off of the momentum of success and discover how to leverage it even further.
- **What current business environment trends might impact our business?**
  - ~ What's changing? Any surprises?
  - ~ Are trends going in the direction we anticipated at our last planning point?
  - ~ Any early indicators of shifts: values, customer behavior, social, economic?
- **Sort out trends that might provide opportunity in the marketplace.**
- **Sort out trends that might indicate threats in the marketplace.**
- **Candidly identify weaknesses and strengths.**
  - ~ How do the weaknesses and strengths align with the threats and opportunities?
- **What big ideas do we have about keeping our business valuable & vibrant?**
- **Is additional information or research needed to make strategic decisions?**
- **In light of the above discussion, does our mission remain relevant?**
- **Prioritize threats and weaknesses.**
- **Prioritize opportunities.**
- **Select five to seven items from the priorities list for strategic attention.**
- **Outline plans around targeted opportunities: tactics, resources, milestones and measures.**
- **Articulate how this plan aligns with existing vision or creates a new vision.**

119

Board Annual Planning Cycle

Month 1: Board and key executives spend 1.5 – 2 days in strategic planning activity resulting in draft architecture of a vision, strategic directions, and tactics.

Month 2-3: Executive team and board follow-up additional research, tactical organization, timing, and decisions to formalize a strategic action plan.

Month 4: Executive team and board reviews details of tactical plan and board approves strategic objectives, resources, milestones and accountabilities.

Months 5+: Board agenda reflects Strategic Plan:
- 50-75 percent of agenda discusses strategy, relevance, and progress.
- Each and every item on the business agenda can be linked to the strategic plan in some manner.
- New data or sudden changes in the business environment are noted and discussed relative to the strategic objectives.

Month 6: Board identifies dates and commitments for follow-up strategic planning session in month 12:
- Anticipates length of planning retreat.
  - ~ one day for current plan working well.
  - ~ longer if significant business shifts have occurred.
- Identifies data that will be needed for the planning process.
- Secures high impact facilitator as resource.

Month 10:   Pre-survey of board on strategic plan is used to prepare for planning retreat.

Month 12:   Board strategic planning retreat (see "Strategic Planning Meeting Process Agenda" following).

Sample Strategic Planning Meeting Process Agenda

"If the early 21st Century is teaching us one thing,
it is to be cautious about the word impossible!"

Activity	Outcome
I. Global environmental scan of trends and issues potentially relevant to business success. environment.	Big picture view of business long term
II. Specific identification of trends and issues in our business sector environment.	Highlight and focus trends and issues.
III. Identification of business threats and weaknesses.	Identify vulnerabilities.
IV. Identification of potential opportunities within business environment.	Focused identification of opportunities.
V. Big ideas: innovative and out of the box thinking "Boldly imagine our enterprise five years out."	Assure creativity in the plan.

[NOTE: Boards may frequently use a pre-survey to capture the thoughts on the above questions so as to reserve as much retreat time as possible for dialogue.]

VI. Identification of information and data gaps. What information do we need to best determine priorities and our courses of action?	Assure data based planning activities.

VII. Revisiting "mission" just in case it's shifting.   Assuring relevance.

VIII. Prioritization of threats and weaknesses.   Focus efforts.

IX.   Prioritization of opportunities.   Focus efforts.

X.   Outline action planning around   Implementation
      targeted threats and weaknesses.   Planning.

XI.   Outline action planning around targeted   Implementation
      opportunities priorities.   Planning.

CHAPTER 7

Governance Leadership Succession and Recruitment

"In the future, high performance boards will likely require board candidates to complete some governance precertification as a requirement to serve."

It's now commonplace for boards to expect CEOs to have a leadership succession plan. It should also be commonplace for boards to have a well-defined process and investment in their own governance leadership succession.

For appointed boards this is no more complex a challenge than assuring clear board agreement on the desired board makeup profile and initiating early identification of potential board members. By identifying potential candidates early and engaging them in some manner in the organization it is possible to obtain a better idea of their competencies and level of commitment.

For boards where memberships elect board members in some manner the leadership succession formula is more complicated. Being unable to dictate the next generation of board member, the board is left to find other means of assuring capable candidates choose to run for office. The ideal way is for the board to have a clearly identified set of expected competencies (not simply years of service to the organization) and offer regular governance training around those competencies throughout their membership. This process improves the odds that a future candidate has at least been exposed to principles of governance and taken their own inventory of how their competencies align. I'm now working with association boards who may soon begin requiring potential candidates to pre-certify specific governance literacy in order to qualify for the ballot.

Whatever your commitment to the quality of future governance, the following ideas will make for lively conversation.

Governance Leadership Succession

Leadership succession planning of management has been on the radar screen for boards of directors for more than a decade. Envisioning the great baby boomer retirement cliff and needing to be generally prepared for a CEO to leave has been cause for most organizations to have a succession discussion about both replacement possibilities. It's now common for larger organizations to have an active leadership succession planning process and a developmental architecture to support it extending deep into the organization's structure.

However, the board itself has been missing from the succession thinking. Although it's common to have discussions about officer succession and "chair elect" positions a year ahead, the overall strategic thinking about identifying, attracting and developing new board members before they're needed remains a gap in contemporary governance practice. Simply asking current board members who they know is a shallow and less robust means of identifying the true leadership you might need for the future.

In my experience, high-performance governance practice involves identifying possible new board members three to five years out and finding ways to engage them, confirm their commitment and develop their governance leadership competency before any board openings occur. This can be accomplished with boards who appoint their own members as well as with association or credit union boards who require board elections for additions to the board. Many boards consider having non-board members on committees as their succession pool. I believe this is insufficient and suggest there be a more formal and inclusive process.

What might this process look like?

Profile your board competencies

Governance leadership succession starts with a profile of the competencies important for effective governance leadership of your organization. This makes the identification, development and selection process more focused rather than a shotgun approach. Yes, you may shift some of your ideal profile over the years. However, core competencies of effective board members are well identified in the literature and should be your primary target. At Counterpart International, a board upon which I've served as Governance Committee Chair, we've created a "profile matrix" of key board competency and experience makeup to help guide our recruitment. This allows us to visually track on-board competencies such as finance, strategy, fundraising, international business and governance for example.

Develop your prospects

Let's look at the odds I've observed from experience with more than 300 boards of directors. If you start with a pool of 30 potential prospects that meet your ideal board profile you'll end up three years later with about three to five who have sustained interest and commitment to development and for whom you've been able to confirm competencies. Elevations Credit Union in Boulder, Colorado, began this with 17 names on the prospect list. Eighteen months later the list was down to two candidates the board felt comfortable encouraging to run for the board. At Counterpart International, we began two years ago with about 25 prospects identified by staff, executive team, board and past board members and have just recently added four top notch board members who fit our profile needs and who have passion for our work. Taking time with this prospecting process helps provide greater confidence in your final selections or nominations.

Where do you find prospects?

Early identification of potential board members is one of the greatest board challenges. Certainly the gadflies who volunteer for anything in your organization or the egocentric who desires a board seat for the wrong reasons are not your target group. Ask yourself these questions:

If you're an association

Where have you seen some authentic servant leadership out in the states and regions? Further explore the capabilities of these folks. The American

Association of Nurse Anesthetists targets its state "President-Elect" group for a governance boot camp every year. It also sponsors annual governance training for new committee members as well as hosting a "Fall Leadership Academy" where any member can come learn about effective governance. These touches encourage members to consider board service while raising the governance literacy of a large inclusive pool of prospects.

If you're a not-for-profit

Where might the type of leadership potential you seek congregate? Colleges/universities? Chambers of Commerce? Professional associations? Young professional groups? In my state, the Colorado Black Chamber of Commerce and Latino Chamber of Commerce are great sources of potential leadership. In other communities, Asian and Native American Chambers of Commerce expand a potential pool of leadership diversity for a board to consider. It's entirely possible a prospect may be found in any of these sectors who does not currently have but can see a passion in your work and eventually wish to serve.

What younger leaders have you run across who you might put into the mix?

Most every board is looking for younger members these days, and trying to specifically target the 20-40-year olds. Yes, plenty of them have mature leadership capabilities beyond the traditional inexperienced stereotype. The Virginia Nurses Association scanned its membership statewide to identify its "40 Under 40" future leaders group and engage them in ongoing leadership and governance education and involvement in statewide strategies. This has resulted in its ability to add one much younger board member to its mix—and she's fantastic!

Must you know personally someone to invite them into your prospect cadre?

No. Scanning your population universe for potential candidates is hard work but does turn up fresh prospects. Even when the dean at the local business school may not be interested now, she will most certainly have a referral or two for you to consider.

How might you test commitment while growing governance competencies?

Ask! Invite prospects to become involved at some level of your organization. Focus group participation, volunteering at an event or serving on a task force gets their feet wet and allows their decision-making process to sort through their interest in your organization. At the same time, you're viewing the potential prospect's fit with your organization. If you hold state, regional or national meetings, conduct some governance leadership training at every one attended by 50 people or more. For every committee or task force insert governance leadership training into its processes—a little dose over a year's period makes a difference. The Board of Certification for Athletic Trainers has conducted "mini governance" lessons at every committee meeting for several years. As you size down your original list to a smaller pool engage them on committees and include them in strategic planning and other organizational events to hone their literacy of how you currently do business. This immersion will also help you further determine their level of commitment.

Use a rigorous selection process

A rigorous selection process begins with a statement of interest and finishes with a face-to-face interview with the full board. In the process, require prospects to speak to their specific governance competencies and education. Strategic planning, financial oversight, enterprise management, political savvy and leading transformations are all currently central to successful governance.

I'm currently working with a large national professional association on the possibility of creating a "voluntary governance certification" program to be required prior to accepting a nomination to run for a director's position. While this pre-certification process is a new and controversial idea today I predict it will be more commonplace by 2015.

Who takes charge of a governance leadership succession process? The board governance or nominating committee should sponsor and oversee the process. Frequently one committee member and the CEO will conduct a first round of background screening and personal interviews as part of the committee's efforts to hone a list of prospects to a smaller list of serious candidates. A final round of competency and interest confirmation should be conducted by the chairperson and a committee person. In the end, a face-to-face interaction with the full board should determine final candidate status.

High-performance board members of all ages are out there who can raise the governance leadership competency of your whole board. Following a structured, methodical and strategic process for recruiting new board members will result in a higher performing board of directors to lead your organization into the future.

High performance boards:

(1) Have a clearly identified profile for a desired board member.
(2) Have identified a cadre of potentials two to three years in advance of needing to appoint them.
(3) Have at least 2-3 high potential candidates they are currently engaging and grooming for a near term vacancy.

TABLE 8

Governance Leadership Succession Scenario

20 potential individuals identified will result in 10 who will step up at least once on behalf of the organization.	5 will be willing to make a more engaged commitment.	2–3 will be ready and willing to compete for board consideration.	Well-developed and recruited board member joins the board!
Typical Engagement: ❑ Focus group. ❑ Short-term task force. ❑ Assistance with events. ❑ Non-board committee member.	**Typical Engagement:** ❑ Focus group. ❑ Short-term task force. ❑ Assistance with events. ❑ Non-board committee member. ❑ Participation in board leadership development.	**Typical Engagement:** ❑ Serious commitment to organizational support and involvement. ❑ Participation in board leadership development. ❑ Possibly a non-voting "associate" board position or "Blue Ribbon Advisory Board" member.	Commitment made to full board engagement.
Who Knows These Folks? Scan your field of enterprise for outstanding leaders. Board and staff identify names. Inquire of your professional network.	**Not all of these folks will be willing or desirable to make the next cut.** Demonstrated engagement and commitment as well as "fit" with desired board competencies is used as a selection filter here.	**Commitment to serve and learn defines this group.** At this point you're anticipating a future appointment and should reward commitment with support for learning and invitations for full engagement with the current board and organizational leaders.	These board members will commit to finding and developing the next generation of board members!

Perspective on an Ideal Board Competency Mix

"Selecting governance leadership by any measure other than leadership competencies is an outdated governance model."

TABLE 9

Ideal Board Competency Mix

3 Younger Professionals	3 Business-Savvy/ Seasoned Management Leaders	3 High-Profile Community, State, National, International Leaders
Selected from professionals in your field of enterprise for outstanding leadership potential.	Identified from broad recruitment efforts with constituencies and professional networks.	Leaders with advanced governance, political or executive leadership experience highly regarded in your community of interest.
Competencies: ■ Personal integrity. ■ Interpersonally adept. ■ Active learner. ■ Technology literate. ■ Passion and commitment to volunteer leadership.	**Competencies:** ■ Enterprise management. ■ Planning. ■ Marketing. ■ Financially literate. ■ Group leadership. ■ Change management. ■ Innovative.	**Competencies:** ■ Strategic thinking. ■ Political savvy. ■ Governance leadership. ■ Leading transformation. ■ Partnerships.

Board Youth Movement as seen by some CEOs and Board members

© MARK ANDERSON, WWW.ANDERTOONS.COM

"In a word, waaaaaaah."

THE BLUE RIBBON ADVISORY BOARD
An alternative avenue of support

A group of leaders passionate about your enterprise and its mission but not free to commit to full board service because of other commitments or personal lifestyle. They will still respond to calls for advice, attend a planning session once or twice a year and pick up the phone to help you connect with resources. This is the place for big name busy people who wish to support you!

Recruiting Younger Board Members

I conducted a recent seminar for 100 board members and at least half of the boards represented had a membership goal in their strategic plan to target and serve younger customers, members or constituents. This same group also had a strategic goal to recruit younger board members—generally targeted as 40 years old or younger. As a perspective on the aging of boards, table 9 below summarizes the 2012 data from BoardSource and the Filene Institute about board membership in the nonprofit and Credit Union arena.

TABLE 10

Age	Represented on Nonprofit Boards	Represented on C.U. Boards
Under 30 years	2%	1%
30–39 years	12%	5%
40–49 years	29%	17%
50–64 years	43%	+/-38%
65+ years	14%	+/-39%

As you can see, bringing down average board age is a challenge across all areas of governance.

Targeting younger people for your board is generally not a controversial topic in governance. Whenever I bring it up in my seminars most everyone agrees it would be a good idea: "_but_," they say, "it's so difficult to find the talent needed and the commitment to serve." I certainly understand the challenge. However, I find boards that make a serious commitment to go find younger potential board members make it happen. Yes, there are professionals 30-40 years old, well qualified to serve on boards—I know. I just helped recruit two 30-year-olds to an international board on which I serve.

Where to start?

Get a commitment from your board that they will seriously support candidacy from younger people who have the credentials to serve. Try to keep from putting too many "ifs, ands, or buts" on your commitment. The candidates don't need to have previously served on one of your committees or volunteered with you in some capacity. Talent is talent and plenty of qualified folks would be happy to serve on your board. I know, I help make this happen every year.

Make it known to your customer service representatives or field staff that you are looking for someone generally between 21 and 40 years old who might have a business or professional background. Maybe they run their own business, are in management somewhere, or as a professional they are active in a network like the Chamber of Commerce or some other community or professional group. Your reps and field staff deal with these folks every day and know who they are. Maybe provide a contest for generating leads upon which the board might follow-up.

As a board, brainstorm not who you know; brainstorm who you know who might know of a younger community leader like the one you're looking for. Your networks should generate plenty of names for screening. At this early phase, don't worry about "scratching" a name from the list, worry about generating a big list—try to get at least thirty names. From this big list you'll likely find one to two candidates your board will be happy to engage. If indeed you're trying to affirm diversity on your board then searching in some of the places listed below will help.

Where might you find qualified younger board members?

- College and university faculty and graduate students.
- Chambers of Commerce.
- Specialty Chamber groups: Black, Latino, Asian, Native American.
- Young Professional groups.
- Professional associations.
- Small Business Alliance groups.
- Specialty legal societies.

- State non-profit societies.
- Mid-to upper managers of businesses in your area.

In general, leadership succession or "board refresh" has become a hot topic in governance and certainly the conversation around younger board members can generate emotion with talented older trustees. However, there are plenty of mature, talented, experienced people under 40 who would love to help lead your organization. They won't necessarily come to you—if you're serious you must go to them. For more detail on a discipline of recruiting future board members, please see my article at **www.signatureresources.com**, in the Governance Leadership section: "Governance Leadership Succession."

Reflection

Despite the board's confidence in your current makeup, how might you begin thinking about the competencies that might add value in your next appointment?

Might you use your next appointments to broaden the diverse makeup of your board?

Is having "associate" board members—non-voting but participating members—a leadership succession strategy with which your board would feel comfortable?

TABLE 11

Typical Board Profile Worksheet

Dimensions	Current Members	Prospective Candidates
Age		
Under 21		
22–35		
36–45		
46–55		
56–65		
Over 65		
Gender		
Female		
Male		
Ethnicity		
African American/Black		
Asian/Pacific Islander		
Caucasian/White		
Hispanic/Latino		
Native American/Indian		
Other		
Competencies		
Leading complex enterprise		
Finance and budget		
Strategic thinking/planning		
Organizational transformation		
Policy leadership		
Governance		
Entrepreneurship		
Fundraising		
Advocacy		
Community Connections		
Business entities		
Education		
Healthcare		
Government		
Community services		
Religious entities		
Media		
Philanthropy		
Other		
Prior years of engagement with your organization?		

Are You Ready for the Boardroom?

The 2012 BoardSource "Nonprofit Governance Index tells us "40 percent of nonprofit board members don't really understand what they are supposed to do." Possibly your board has encountered this uncertainty among new board members.

You may already have a board member "job description" on your web site, including expected time commitments. You may also have posted a bibliography of relevant governance literature with which new board members should become familiar. Online information is becoming commonly available, as is a list of competencies and backgrounds the organization seeks in a new board member.

You might wish to consider adding the general guidance below as a means of helping future board members seriously reflect upon their readiness and commitment to serve.

The little things:

- I am willing to give the organization my best regardless of recognition or reward.

- I am able to commit to at least 150 hours of board service annually without feeling burdened.

- I am willing to commit to at least 24 hours a year developing my governance literacy and capabilities.

- I understand business financial systems and can interpret a balance sheet.

- I am technologically literate enough to navigate the Internet, social media, and the Microsoft suite of software products without assistance.

- I am assertive enough to not be intimidated yet authentic enough to be an appreciative listener.

- I have studied materials on the responsibilities of a governing board and understand the difference between the board's role and management's role.

- I understand I may be asked to fundraise or advocate on behalf of our organization and am comfortable with those roles.

- I recognize I'm here to serve our constituent's best interests.

The big things:

- I recognize I am a legal trustee of the significant value our constituents are counting on us to deliver.

- I understand the conditions of our corporate or nonprofit corporate and IRS status.

- I understand I don't represent a gender, ethic, socio-economic, regional, age related, or other demographic group—I represent all our constituents.

- I'm a learner and commit to constantly improve my perspective and skills.

- I am committed to assuring our board receives substantial and timely feedback regarding our customer, member or constituents perceptions, needs and desires relative to our organization.

- I will seek out an experienced board member—within or external to our board—to provide mentor support during my service.

- If I don't understand materials or decisions brought to the board I will persevere with questions until I am satisfied.

- I'm familiar with some of the most recent literature on the challenges of governance and standards of good governance.

- I can facilitate a team of diverse others in cooperative problem solving.

- I am known for thinking innovatively and embracing new ideas and concepts and am willing to challenge our board to stretch their thinking.

- I'm well -read enough to understand the pace of and need for change, and the degree of risk present in today's business environment.

- I am motivated to continually look to the future horizon for new ideas and approaches and will assure they emerge in our agendas.

- I understand the conflict of interest restrictions of board service.

- I commit to finding someone more experienced and competent than me to recruit for board service.

- After a reasonable amount of board service I'll be willing to move aside for new board members.

If I really wish to be governance ready day one I will read all of the following:

BoardSource. Twelve Principles of Governance That Power Exceptional Boards (2005)
Charan, Ram. Owning UP: the 14 Questions Every Board Member Needs to Ask (2009)
Chait, Richard, et. al. Governance as Leadership (2004)
Sonnenfeld, Jeffrey, et. al. "What CEOs Really Think of Their Boards," Harvard Business Review (4/2013)

Ten Questions that make Boards Better

Simple questions, regular discussions, ongoing tutorials: these basics help even the most experienced board members stay focused on their governance responsibility. Here's a quick way to look at your board's behavior using three questions of strategy, three questions of performance, and four questions of governance that may help lead you to organizational success.

Regarding Strategy

1. **How well are we meeting our mission?**
    Why do we exist? That's the question a mission statement answers. What evidence does the board review each year to assure its fulfilling it purpose? Does the board check annually to assure that mission hasn't shifted or, more importantly, should shift? Changing business affiliations, economics and community conditions can lead to shifts in your reason to exist.

2. **What opportunities or threats are being presented in our changing business environment?**
    Traditional "strategic planning" processes ask boards to assess the changes in their business environment and conduct a "SWOT" analysis of how well they are aligned for success. SWOT represents strengths, weaknesses, opportunities and threats that an organization faces in navigating its business environment. If surprise challenges and issues keep popping up during the year, your board might wish to revisit your investment in these basics.

3. **What is our three-year plan to become better and stronger?**
    No business environment is ever static. As conditions change, organizations too must change to adapt. Values, technology, economics, employee pools, customer expectations all migrate. The longer-range plan (three to five years) attempts to outline and project the strategies

145

and tactics needed for the organization to remain successful, vibrant, and relevant. This plan should be the subject of each board meeting, generally, at least 50-75 percent of your agenda.

Regarding Performance

4. **How strong and well managed are our finances?**
   What are the few key data points that will give you a clear sense of how the organization is doing with its finances? How well does your board understand the details of budgeting, tracking and financial strategy? Since very few board members, especially in the community and association organizational marketplace, have strong financial management backgrounds, boards should have a plan to help their members grasp the basics of finance. Boards obviously should receive monthly or quarterly reports on financial performance. These reports should be offered in simple and lay language. Boards may also invite their accounting firms to conduct budget tutorials, help them develop reports that make sense, and help them ask the right questions.

5. **How would our customers, members, constituents like to see us change?**
   Board members should receive at least quarterly or bi-annual reports on customer satisfaction and organizational efforts to improve service. Customer value and satisfaction are too important for any organization to leave to anecdotal evidence or rough impressions. Inviting input provides opportunity to better meet your mission, identify quality improvement opportunity and track shifting customer values and expectations. This information usually comes from surveys, focus groups, or customer feedback posted on blogs or to your organization's web site.

6. **Are our employees satisfied and fully engaged in our work?**
   Customer satisfaction is dependent on the quality of the work environment. It's a challenge for dissatisfied employees, facing poor leadership and chaotic work processes, to satisfy customers. At least once

a year the board should receive staff feedback data about the organizational work environment from tools like "employee engagement" or "organizational climate surveys." These tools will help assess the type of leadership climate being set and help identify issues to which the CEO should attend.

Regarding Governance

7. **Are we governing, managing, or rubber-stamping?**
   For whatever reason, many board members fail to fully engage and challenge the recommendations and decisions brought before them. In the opposite direction, too many board members attempt to delve deeply into dictating tactics more appropriate for the CEO or others who manage the organization. Governance is about setting policy, organizational direction, approving a budget and plan for delivering its mission and then holding the CEO accountable for accomplishment. Specifying "micro" behaviors is not governance-setting direction, overall policy and boundaries and holding people accountable is.

8. **How can we become more informed and effective?**
   The most effective boards engage in regular self-assessment of their performance and provide broad as well as individualized learning support to raise member's governance competency. Such self-assessments facilitate each board member's opportunity for self-directed learning and encourage appropriate involvement. Some portion of every board meeting should also be invested in board development. Read and discuss a governance article, invite in a local expert, have a key manager come in and provide a deep explanation of their department.

9. **Who have we identified and begun grooming to replace departing board members?**
   Board vacancies, some of which are unplanned, frequently lead to a period of frantic discussion about who might be an appropriate

replacement appointment. Progressive boards have a succession plan in place. A succession plan should provide early identification of leaders with board potential and some ongoing development and engagement with them to facilitate governance maturation. The quality of the board make-up is far too important to leave to last minute searches.

10. **Does the board revisit, clarify and provide feedback on the CEO's performance at least twice a year?**
    Boards hire the chief executive officer to manage, lead, and administer their enterprise. An effective board CEO relationship requires clear objectives and expectations. Timely feedback is enhanced by having a twice-a-year appointment to discuss performance. Typical CEO feedback should cover leadership, overall organizational performance, community and government relations, board relations, and any specific performance objectives previously identified. The entire board should be involved in this assessment, not just the executive committee.

Ten Strategies that Make Boards More Effective

1. **Use a "balanced measures" approach to track organizational performance**
    Organizations in the last decade have adopted a "balanced measures" approach to judging performance. Business results have always been prominent. Now progressive organizations also measure customer, member, constituent value and employee engagement. Balance is a relative term. The three measures: business results, customer performance, and employee engagement, are linked to one another so closely in the business literature that keeping a close eye in each of the categories provides boards a full-spectrum view of enterprise performance.

2. **Create a simple set of dashboard indicators to review at each meeting.**
    Balanced measures require a reporting system that can be grasped easily and reported with monthly or quarterly frequency. The "dashboard" metaphor suggests how boards should require performance information to be presented: a simple set of indicators provides a quick "eye" on overall performance and allows boards to determine where and when they wish more detailed reports. How many "dials" should the board review? Somewhere in the neighborhood of 3-7 for each balanced measure. Just the process of identifying and developing the dashboard is a great board development exercise.

3. **Tie at least 50-75 percent of each agenda to the objectives of your strategic plan.**
    Most board meetings are a fast-paced run through of old and new business and the traditional boring report-outs from administrators. With a balanced measures approach you can simplify the time required for report-outs; with a consent agenda approach (see "Consent Agenda" in the Support Materials section) you can accept numerous self evident

update reports without wasting valuable board time. That leaves about half an agenda for one of the most important functions of governance: strategic thinking and planning. In today's fast changing business environment, boards struggle to assure enough strategic change to remain relevant and successful. Investing at least half of each meeting to strategy discussions enhances focus, performance, and responsiveness to strategic issues.

4. **Conduct board development at each board meeting.**
Board development is a constant challenge for most organizations. Limitations on budgets and free time make travel and conference participation for education a rare opportunity. One solution is to do a wee bit of development at each board meeting. Reading and discussing an article on governance, scheduling product or service tutorials at each meeting, having a local person who is "seasoned" at governance provide a short tutorial on a chosen topic, asking your accountant to deliver a financial lesson (e.g. how to read a balance sheet), having a customer visit and provide their explanation of your product or service value are all brief time investments that will contribute to growth of governance capabilities.

5. **Have a brief product or service tutorial at each board meeting.**
A 10 to 15 minute update on one of your organization's products or services can provide a means for board members to stay current and maintain a "feel" for the texture of their enterprise. This enhanced literacy is also accompanied by a chance to interact briefly with managers and program leaders as a means of evaluating the CEO's management and leadership influence. These briefings (15 minutes is sufficient) also qualify as board development.

6. **Create "rules of engagement" for interaction and support of one another.**
A seasoned board is adept at decision making, interpersonal relationships and dealing with difference of opinion and conflict.

Unfortunately, most of us don't serve with a full contingent of experienced governance members. Most groups, intending to behave more like teams, find it helpful to develop a set of rules of engagement that outlines commitments expected from each board member (see "Board of Directors Rules of Engagement" in Support Materials section).

7. **Have a job description and commitment to serve signed by each member.**

   Joining a board is frequently fraught with uncertainty about the time commitment required, conflict of interest guidelines, board development commitments, travel, representation, and other board duties. Just like a job description helps focus an employee's work, a board job description not only helps focus the reality of the commitment but also scares away those who might consider joining the board for the wrong reasons. Making the job description and conflict of interest statement a commitment that each new board member signs helps raise the awareness of the expected governance commitments.

8. **Conduct a board self-assessment at least once a year.**

   Progressive boards engage in regular self-assessments. These can be as limited or far ranging as the board feels is helpful based on its support capacity. It's critical for boards to do some form of self assessment each year, even if the board chooses not to conduct a large scale, more cumbersome assessment. For example, many boards conduct annual, focused assessments of the quality of meetings, agenda management, or perceptions of individual participation. While such comprehensive assessment would cover all aspects of governance, boards may be better-served to schedule such a full-scale assessment every several years while selecting some portions for focus on an annual basis (see three sample assessments in the Support Materials section).

9. **Provide formal feedback to your CEO twice a year.**

   While CEO evaluation and goal setting is an annual function required in effective governance, many boards fail to do it on a timely basis.

151

Even when conducted effectively, the annual review is not enough: a formal mid year review should also occur that provides the CEO direct, formal feedback on how the board sees performance. This bi-annual discussion keeps expectations and performance calibrated, assures CEOs have timely recognition of board perceptions, and will result in better overall organizational and board performance. If the board and CEO are not fully in sync, quarterly discussions may be called for. While the once a year evaluation and goal setting will be time-consuming, the mid-year feedback process will customarily require less time investment, especially if performance is on track. Customarily the executive or governance committee leads the evaluation and review process, however, all board members should be involved in the process.

10. **Retreat at least once a year to revisit and reflect on organizational values and strategic plans.**
    The progressive board finds time to retreat at least once a year, if only for a day, away from the pressures of a typical agenda. Discussion at these retreats allows relaxed exploration of changing business conditions, shifting customer expectations, chronic challenges, expansion, and a renewal of focus on strategy for the governance body. An annual strategic planning retreat is almost commonplace with many boards. Certainly, some effort to refresh the strategic plan at least every three years is a minimum. In our experience the average retreat is somewhere around 1.5 days, but it is not unheard of to invest a single day or to expand to 2.5 - 3 days for boards facing more complex challenges. Whatever your investment, make it count. Creating a calendar that selects the time a year in advance gives most board members time to clear their calendar and make the commitment.

Simple Financial Questions for Not-for-Profit Board Members

Co-authored with Nancy Pindus, MBA, CPA

At the risk of oversimplifying financial oversight we offer the following 10 basic questions to increase your ability to know what you need to understand to be a good board member.

1. **Where are our sources of revenue?**

   An engaged board member should understand the major sources of income for the organization and their historical patterns. The source for this information is the Income Statement, also called the Statement of Activities. Typically, boards receive a monthly or quarterly report at each meeting with current year, month, and last year and month data. When you understand where the money comes from to fund the activities of the organization then you can inquire as to "why" the grant, dues revenue, contract, or sale is valuable to the funding source or customer.

2. **Where do we spend money?**

   What are the major expense categories and what has been their historical performance? For many service organizations "labor" and "benefits" constitute the biggest expense categories. For organizations with a manufacturing process raw materials, production, and delivery constitute the biggest categories. The source for this information is the Income Statement, also known as the Statement of Activities, usually under the "expense" heading. For all organizations the costs of administration and management need to be monitored to assure they are not out of line with industry benchmarks, donor expectations, etc.

3. **What are our overall assets and liabilities?**
    Customarily this can be determined in the Balance Sheet, also know as the Statement of Financial Position. This provides important information about the organization's ability to meet short-term and long-term obligations, including operating expenses and interest on debt.

4. **What's our operating reserve?**
    This is the money we have saved for emergencies. Most experts suggest it should be at minimum the amount it would take to pay all of your bills for three months. A more conservative level of safety is probably an amount equivalent to six to twelve months of operating expenses. Organizations with limited operating reserve are at greater risk of not being able to continue business should a disaster hit such as lost sales or contract, market share lost to competitors or other impacts which might reduce income streams.

5. **How have our overall financials changed since a year (or three or five years) ago?**
    Understanding a historical perspective can help you see the bigger picture of seasonal income and expense, impacts of program or strategic change, and provide a baseline from which to watch current numbers and ask better questions.

6. **What's the potential to sustain or increase revenue from current sources?**
    How secure are our current sources of revenue? Grants and contracts with expiration and re-compete dates require advanced thinking to assure healthy cash flows are maintained. What's happening in the market place that might affect our ability to re-compete for grants or contracts or add on additional work and services? Products and services always change in value to the customer. What does our market and customer research tell us about changing value?

7. **What's the potential to generate revenue from new sources?**
    Strategic planning affects financial management in the following way: by regularly looking at how the business environment is shifting you can better anticipate new opportunities developing before they are imminent. By constantly looking at what other successful organizations in your marketplace are doing you can get wind of new ideas from some of the market leaders. New products and services always require a lot of financial planning to assure the expenses invested, the cost of delivering and the profitability available on our price are accurate.

8. **Were there any concerns noted in our last external financial audit?**
    The role of the external audit is to give the board of directors confidence in the integrity of the financial accounting of the organization and to identify any risks or non-standard financial practices that require attention. Audits frequently identify "exceptions" in their review. Exceptions are their professional judgment that a financial policy or practice may not meet current and commonly expected accounting practice.

9. **What have our audited financial statements concluded?** The best place for board members to develop a basic comfort level with standard financial statements and a few key financial measures is the organization's audited financial statements. Ideally a new board member might want to look at the past three years of audited financial statements in order to see changes and trends. The audited financial statements consist of five parts:

    (1) The letter. The auditor's letter states the period covered by the financial statements, the methods used and any exceptions or concerns.

    (2) The Income Statement (may also be called the Statement of Operations, Statement of Activities, Statement of Operations and

Changes in Net Assets, Statement of Profit and Loss, Statement of Earnings, Statement of Revenues and Expenses). Regardless of the title used, this statement shows the revenues and expenses for the reporting period, and the change in net assets from the beginning to the end of the reporting period.

(3)   The Balance Sheet (also called the Statement of Financial Position) shows both current (in the reporting period) and long-term assets and liabilities.

(4)   The Cash Flow Statement (also called the Cash Flow from Operations) shows the beginning and ending cash balance for the organization for the reporting period and the transactions (e.g., depreciation, losses, changes in assets and liabilities) that affected cash balance.

(5)   The Footnotes. Seriously, these are not as technical (or as boring) as you might think. The footnotes often include descriptive information about the organization, its ownership, the restricted assets, donated materials, investments, property and depreciation.

10. What does the federal Sarbanes-Oxley legislation mean for our Board?

Created to rebuild public trust in the corporate community in the wake of corporate and accounting scandals, the federal legislation that has become known as the Sarbanes-Oxley Act, signed into law on July 30, 2002, requires publicly traded companies to conform to new standards in financial transactions and audit procedures. While nearly all of the provisions of the "Act" apply only to publicly traded corporations, the passage of the bill served as a wake-up call to the entire nonprofit community. Nonprofit leaders should look carefully at the provisions of Sarbanes-Oxley, as well as their state laws, and determine whether their organizations ought to voluntarily adopt governance best practices, even if not mandated by law. A good source for more information is **http://www.independentsector.org/PDFs/sarbanesoxley.pdf**.

Key financial practices for boards to address are:

- **Conduct outside audits**. Rotate the auditor or lead partner at least every five years. Avoid any conflict of interest in staff exchange between the audit firm and the organization. Don't use the auditing firm for non-auditing services except tax form preparation without pre-approval from the audit committee.
- **Establish a separate audit committee of the board** to select and oversee the auditing company and review the audit. Assure that the committee is independent and financially competent.
- **Review and certify financial statements.** The CEO and CFO should sign off on all financial statements (either formally or in practice), including IRS Form 990, to ensure they are accurate, complete, and filed on time. The board should review and approve financial statements and IRS Form 990 tax returns for completeness and accuracy. **Starting in 2009 "IRS Form 990" asks questions regarding board independence and oversight.** [See: www.nono.com/legal-encyclopedia/article—30274]
- **Avoid Conflict of Interest.** Personal loans should not be made to directors and executives. The board should adopt a conflict of interest policy and a regular and rigorous means of enforcing it. Board conflict of interest statements should be signed each year.
- **Strive for greater disclosure and transparency to donors, public officials, the media, and others.** Disclose Form 990 and 990-PF in a current and easily accessible way (also required of all nonprofit organizations by IRS law), including moving to electronic filing of Form 990 and 990-PF. Disclose audited financial statements.
- **Protect whistle blowers.** Develop, adopt, and disclose a formal process to deal with complaints and prevent retaliation.

- **Follow rules for document retention and destruction.** Have a written, mandatory document retention and periodic destruction policy, which includes guidelines for electronic files and voicemail.

While a number of these provisions pertain to internal operations of the organizations, remember that board members are responsible for oversight, including assuring the recommended polices and practices are in place.

Marketing Facts Every Board Should Know

We all market: products, services, philanthropy, image and brand. Some boards must face a more comprehensive strategy and investment in marketing than others. Marketing, however, is not as simple as it appears and is certainly more complex than most board members have had a chance to learn about. The notes that follow are a concise, high level attempt to help your board of directors understand the dynamics of marketing, ask the right questions, and establish the right support and direction.

1. **Market based planning is different from marketing**. And both of these differ from sales. Market based planning is the foundation upon which marketing (promotion) and sales (demonstrating a value proposition to a customer) are based. Market based planning means analyzing your market space thoroughly by looking at overall size, your market share, market segments, competitors and how customers make purchasing decisions about your offering. Has your organization articulated the specific elements of your market space addressing the questions noted below?

2. **Who are your targeted market segments?** No marketing approach benefits from a go after everyone shotgun approach. Targeted marketing means you've zeroed in on your highest potential customer base(s) and customized messages and promotion to that segment. Different market segments discover offerings differently, attend to different media, and congregate in different spaces. Can your leadership team describe your targeted market segments and speak specifically to how they behave in the marketplace?

3. **What competitors are in your targeted market space?** Competitive analysis is critical to polishing your messages, offerings and pricing. Knowing who is competing for your business and how they operate

in your market space helps boards of directors provide better quality strategic guidance and approve more sound marketing strategies and budgets. Does your organization have a competitive analysis summarized in a few pages of overview? Is this updated and presented to the board annually?

4. **What do you know about how your market segment makes purchase decisions?** Understanding customer behavior, specifically how customers choose between products of competing value, helps you craft the value of your offering and understand when to make changes in the offering. Understanding what's called the "customer value proposition" is crucial for sustaining your business. What is the real value a customer seeks in your product? What need might your product or service be fulfilling? This can be utility, personal branding and credentialing, cost savings, professional commitment or any number of other "values." Customer surveys are helpful not simply as a measure of service satisfaction but also as a measure of customer value. Remember, customer value propositions change as products and services innovate, economies and demographics shift and competitors enter or leave your marketplace. What two-or-three sentences describe the value proposition of your offering?

5. **How does your market segment use your product/service?** When customers obtain your service or product, how do they utilize it? This is part of the value proposition. Lawn mowers, toothbrushes and tax preparation are easy. Professional credentials, educational services, and memberships are more difficult to determine. Knowing the key features a customer utilizes in your product or service, and how that might be changing with demographic, sociological, technological changes in your marketplace helps boards understand when and how to innovate? Every product or service has a lifecycle of value based upon its utilitarian value to the customer. Product features valuable today may be less valuable as customers' needs change. Boards should

understand how product and service lifecycle is maturing in order to support a timely refresh of your offerings.

6. **How did you arrive at pricing?** Many of the above questions inform the answer to this question. Value, competition, scarcity, niche, economic situation of your customers all play in the pricing formula. Are your offerings a commodity (readily available from other less costly vendors) or a premium (your value and offering is very different)? Think "Super Market Brand" versus "Starbucks" coffee. Do you compete on price or value? Can you unbundle features of your offering so that customers can upgrade purchases along a chain of value? Think telephone services here. Do you want basic? Family plan? Internet access? Each value is priced differently. Knowledge of your competitor's offerings and customer value perception helps boards feel comfortable they are priced right in the marketplace. Sometimes you simply have to test the proposition by experimenting with pricing, using a focus group for feedback on pricing, or strategically deciding to be a value leader or a commodity provider.

7. **What channels are most appropriate for reaching your market segments?** Different market segments pay attention to different channels of communication and media. Ronco still advertises knives on the Saturday afternoon movie channels. Cadillac and Apple have liked Super Bowl ads. Auto insurers are moving more advertising to the internet. What's right for your organization's marketing effort depends on the viewing, listening, and channel exposure most aligned with your targeted market segments. Younger groups might find ads on YouTube valuable while older folks might pay close attention to what AARP promotes. Marketing can be expensive. Enough research should go into understanding the behaviors of your targeted market segments that the board can feel comfortable with the promotion channels in which they invest. And, why they might shift over time.

8. **What are our marketing messages?** Channel refers to the media connections we use to reach our targeted customers. Print, electronic, direct mail, web based, social media, displays, etc. are all channels we use to reach our audiences. "Messages" are the verbal and nonverbal symbols we use to create meaning. If you recall the "Apple Computer versus PC Man" ads you get the picture. It's visual and the meaning is all about ease of use. The IPhone and Droid phone ads are all about visually demonstrating universal connectivity with a wow factor. Look on the web site of your competitor and then review your own website (your storefront for customers) to see how your messages compare. Providing a comprehensive and easy-to-use web presence is a message unto itself. What are the other messages you believe customers will pick up from your web site, your convention booth, and your newsletter? Do they seem to be in sync with all the other data about how your targeted customer behaves? This is one area when boards should not try to be experts. Hire a professional communications staffer if you can afford it or a consultant to re-work your messages but please don't start to believe the board can do this.

9. **What major changes are occurring in your market space?** Economic meltdown, job loss, wars, international relations, and government transformation will all impact how our market space behaves. Competitors may fold or merge, targeted markets might change, customer behavior certainly will be impacted, and the ability of the organization to afford marketing campaigns will be tested. While boards should re-look at their market space at least annually, we might be in a near term era where quick quarterly glimpses are advised. What few indicators could your organization easily track? Sales, customer feedback, and competitor behavior are all fairly easily tracked and are immediate signals about shifts occurring in the marketplace. What's your board's set of sentinel dashboard indicators? Are you comfortable they're sufficient to track market space behavior in real time?

10. **What do your best customers say about your products/services?**
    Our best customers represent those who have bought into the value
    proposition of our offering hook, line, and sinker. These customers
    are usually repeat buyers, active in providing feedback, and may even
    help us re-think product innovation. They are also our best bellwether
    indicator of developing early trouble. Staying in close touch with this
    group helps your organization in two very different ways. One, the
    best customers will help you re-design your products to stay relevant
    to the shifting marketplace. Second, as the best customers start drop-
    ping off, or complaining about price or quality, you know there is
    pressure on the whole of your marketplace. Focus groups, social net-
    works of customers, key customer visits, and paying key customers
    for feedback are all important investments in tracking marketplace,
    customer behavior and your value proposition.

As a board member I always wanted to leave a board meeting confident
in our financial operation, ethics, customer connections and strategy. To stay
confident and avoid micromanaging staff about marketing decisions, boards
should expect timely updates that provide fresh answers to the questions
above. Most importantly, any positive or negative movement in market share
and sales should be tracked at least quarterly. These marketing dashboard
indicators can confirm if your market based planning and marketing are
working or may need revisiting.

The Board and Organizational Culture

We are taught as board members to stay focused on policy and strategy governance and not stray below the line into managerial issues. For many board members the biggest challenge of this guidance surfaces around the issue of corporate culture and employee engagement. Every business desires to be a best place to work; many organizations have that goal in their strategic plan. Yet, at what level does a board get involved? What sentinel metrics should a board reasonably track to assure the CEO is delivering on your expectation? What's a board to do when the metrics don't meet expectations? Let's explore these questions to help point your board's behavior in the right direction.

Can the board legitimately define the corporate culture it expects?

Yes it can, and should. Setting "values" for how the organization behaves is a typical part of setting a mission, vision and strategy. It is possible to define the values of a high performing and humane business culture without micromanaging the CEO. It's also possible to have hard data and survey measures of how well the organization walks the talk on the values. The organizational performance research literature tells us that when customer performance starts to decline it's likely employee engagement has been in decline for some time. A board can and should stay on top of this leading indicator. What do you know about your culture?

What and how should metrics be tracked?

The traditional industrial model is to conduct a climate survey, sometimes also known as an opinion survey, once a year. These surveys typically try to affirm there is a climate of trust, integrity, respect, valuing input, coaching and development and open communication at work everyday.

As the concept of measuring "employee engagement" has overtaken the old "satisfaction" survey approach, high performance organizations expect to measure engagement as proof that the business associates see visible signs of the expected cultural values at work. National and international organizations such as Gallup and BlessingWhite have generated substantial research on the value of sustaining a culture of high employee engagement. For example, it's widely proven a highly engaged workforce can outperform a less engaged organization by 20 percent—many studies say up to 40 percent.

The measures of employee engagement do not have to be overly burdensome. Gallup suggests they can get at your organization's level of employee engagement with just 12 questions (the Q12) although they eagerly sell a much larger survey instrument. Many organizations, publicly competing for a "Best Place to Work" award in their state must use a standard annual survey provided by the organization giving the awards.

The critical point of any survey is to be able to focus in on the critical few differentiating metrics that summarize the climate. Gallup's 12 key questions, for example, or an even smaller group that our research has indicated are also safe indicators (A Legacy of 21st Century Leadership, Wallace/Trinka, Chapter VI), e.g., valuing opinions, providing timely feedback, supporting career growth, appreciation.

Over 30 years of surveying and working with surveys I've developed pretty distinct opinions on surveys—size and frequency. The larger, once-a-year survey is good to get into the decimal points of why organizational associates feel certain ways and to break down data by organizational departments.

However, checking in on culture once a year is an old industrial model in a new virtual era. At least twice a year, and possibly as much as four times a year, a smaller, more focused survey can provide timely indicators of organizational climate and employee engagement. Your board should consider having your CEO and personnel team work toward that end. While an annual survey may include all employees and managers, the in-between, short surveys can use smaller, random samples as good indicators of how things are going. You're welcome to see exactly what I recommend on my website (**www.signatureresources.com** under the heading Governance Leadership, "Measuring Employee Engagement"). I only ask that if you decide to use my models you ask permission—I'll grant it.

There are some common questions that almost everyone agrees measure the type of climate most boards' desire. For example: "I would recommend our organization as a great place to work." "I feel I can be successful and grow in this work environment." "I feel supported in my effort to provide customer service excellence." "I clearly know what's expected and get timely feedback on my performance." These (less than five questions) and others make for great quarterly tests of how a climate of engagement is being sustained. Just as every CEO wants timely feedback on how "fiscal capital" is performing, so too should they be as interested in the "human capital" that drives performance.

What if metrics don't meet board expectations for organizational climate?

First, make sure you're very clear on the dynamics expected in your organizational climate. Maybe do some reading as a board or have some board development on this issue to inform you. Secondly, make sure the survey questions or other measures (e.g. turnover, exit interviews, grievances) you use are good indicators of how that climate is being sustained. Then, with confidence in your clarity and metrics a board can be more directive in specifying that the CEO re-double their organizational efforts around some of the values that get low marks.

CEOs are expected to lead an organization to reasonable excellence in fiscal performance, customer value and satisfaction, _and_ organizational climate. It's not meddling in management to indicate to the CEO that you expect efforts to improve performance around some critical metric of organizational climate. It is meddling to tell them how to do it.

Please understand that organizational climate can be impacted by lots of variables. Poor management skills, poor organizational communication, lack of appropriate training, and poor personnel selection skills can all drag down employee engagement. The answer to a lower employee engagement or organizational climate score is usually not "more rah rah." Organizational climate and employee engagement form a complicated mix of variables. Expect your CEO and human resources people to understand that mix, know how to regularly measure it to your satisfaction and know what to do when scores drop below acceptable levels.

Measuring Employee Engagement / Organizational Climate

Differentiating Employee Engagement

Engaged employees are productive employees. In fact, Gallup says engaged teams produce 20 percent more than their non-engaged counterparts. As a board of directors, it's up to you to define the organizational culture and climate you expect. With so much at stake, it's as important as your role in setting fiscal parameters or customer expectations for good performance. Don't know where to start? After more than 30 years experience and research, I can tell you it's simpler than you may think.

My co-author of A Legacy of 21st Century Leadership, Jim Trinka, and I, devoted an entire chapter to his research on the leadership behaviors most directly related to engaging employees. From the Gallup organization's bellwether findings on the components of employee engagement, and its "Q12" set of questions, Dr. Trinka's own in-depth research found five of those questions to be the key differentiators of leader behavior that generates engagement:

- "Do I receive ample appreciation for doing good work?"
- "Do my opinions and input seem to count?"
- "Does someone at work encourage my development?"
- "Do I feel I have opportunities to learn and grow?"
- "Do I receive timely feedback about how I am doing and my progress?"

Look closely at these questions and you'll see the relationship with the immediate supervisor is the critical element an employee uses to determine how much engagement to give.

Survey Measures: Scope and Frequency

If you're one of the many organizations seeking the "Best Place to Work" award in your area, then you've already committed to an annual, full-scope employee survey likely with more than 100 questions. What if I told you that you need to do these only about every four-to-five years? As a board your focus is in the key indicators of a positive organizational culture, as the five questions above demonstrate, not the weeds of the details.

The annual, fuller scope survey has been a valuable management tool and report of "key metrics" for boards of directors to confirm the organization is being led according to the values they have established. However, the once-a-year, full scope survey is an old industrial model in a new virtual era. Progressive organizations have moved to more frequent measures of employee engagement and organizational climate. I favor quarterly, random short surveys on several key indicators of engagement that can be easily reported on a board dashboard.

What five questions might I recommend you ask of a random sample of employees on a quarterly basis?

- "I believe I can be successful with my work."
- "I have opportunity for growth and development."
- "In my work unit my ideas and opinions are respected and appreciated."
- "I am receiving regular helpful feedback and appreciation about my performance."
- "I am getting the organizational information I need to feel a part of our larger team."

Each of these questions gets at drivers from which high levels of employee engagement emerge. As scores go up you are confirming an engaged workplace. As scores go down your executive team may need to do a bit more diagnosis—but at least it has timely warning of trouble.

Simplifying the Annual Survey

If your organization is doing well yet you still wish to confirm the levels of engagement and open the door for improvement I suggest a skinnier survey—my version. Its available on my website at www.signatureresources. com. A combination of specific inquiries and open-ended responses to provide detailed metrics and subjective comments from your associates this has worked well for many organizations with whom I've worked. You're welcome to use it for free. Simply ask permission—I'll grant it.

The Impact of Governance on Organizational Culture

Integrity. A corporate culture that doesn't value integrity is forced to endure too much secrecy, risky behavior, conflicts stemming from differing standards for different people and poor external confidence in the organization. When boards overlook inappropriate behavior in the organization, people soon learn the difference between the written values and the actual code of acceptability. Beyond reproach is the culture you should aim for. How do you communicate this expectation? Assure a strong policy statement, have a whistle blower policy, model the behavior as a board, and expect your CEO to have zero tolerance for internal integrity lapses.

External Awareness. While we're busy delivering on today's organizational promise, it's easy to overlook how expectations and practice are migrating. The landscape in which we work doesn't stand still. Technology is the most vivid example. Yet customer and citizen expectations, global relationships, economies, as well as what our employees value, are also always on the move. Boards assure that the organization keeps an appropriate sentinel on these shifts and that quarterly conversations about shifting external conditions and expectations take place all the way down to work groups.

Sense of Urgency. If the external environment is always moving, guess what, so too should your organization. Waiting too long and reacting with short spurts of heroic leadership is less healthy than leading and expecting change compatibility every day. Ongoing transformation is woven into a culture through leadership that regularly talks about the future and distributes leadership for change down through the organization. Boards should expect the entire organization to be change agents, not just a few key players.

Learning and Development. Because change is constant and we wish to lead a culture of change compatibility, boards must assure ample investment in developing the workforce. Learning organizations don't see training and learning as an expense. They recognize training as an investment that returns with a workforce that knows you care about their growth and is more greatly attuned to the organization's constant challenge to stay relevant and vibrant. Yes, you will grow some folks who will take those capabilities elsewhere. However, in the meantime, you've become recognized for your commitment to people, are getting more discretionary effort from the workforce and are in a position to attract the brightest and best. Remember, the brightest and best always want to be learning.

Dialogue. "Communication" is much too abstract a word to effectively describe a leadership competency or an organizational cultural value. Effective communication in a vibrant high performance organizational culture is recognized by real dialogue, inclusive input and transparency. Dialogue implies deeper conversations rather than information handoffs. Appreciative exploration gives dialogue its power; people see you care and are willing to invest in hearing them out. When boards model this behavior in their meetings, the entire organization picks up on it.

My Opinion Counts. No one likes to feel powerless and unimportant. Giving voice to the diverse wealth of ideas in an organization not only enhances your problem solving and creativity but also instills an ownership in the workforce missing in many organizational cultures. Everyone has good ideas. Boards must expect that the CEO bring them input from across the workforce, customers, and other organizational partners.

Transparency. A defining characteristic of a culture of leadership is openness and transparency of information and decision-making. People want to know what's going on, the reasons behind decisions and what the outlook is, good, bad or ugly. People distrust secrecy in organizations. Boards must set CEO expectations for an open communication climate that shares timely and abundant information.

Innovation. High-performance organizations have a culture of innovation and creativity. It doesn't happen by spontaneous combustion. Governance can set the tone for an organization: will it allow assumptions to be challenged? Is there a spirit of inquiry that's respected and rewarded rather than crushed by the board? Does the workforce perceive they have permission to challenge assumptions, advance new ideas, suggestions and process course corrections? When boards model a spirit of novelty people understand that the organization permits and encourages big ideas and new possibilities. Great CEOs scare their boards on occasion and exceptional boards encourage it.

Collaboration. Most every organization is challenged by its internal silos; the functional or divisional boundaries that can isolate work teams, inhibit effective communication and reduce creativity. High performance cultures demand cross-functional decision making, planning and support. They also set high expectations for external collaboration and partnerships so that the enterprise can be boosted by the talent and intellectual capital outside their walls. Boards model this behavior and hold managers at all levels accountable for collaboration. In a high performance culture, "teamness" is pervasive.

Accountability. By now most everyone has heard of GE's annual process of identifying the bottom 10 per cent of performers in all categories and moving them out of the organization. Well, that is one means of signaling accountability. But boards can also assure organizational accountability by providing clear expectations and regular feedback to the CEO. Organizational human resources policies should assure that coaching and development is abundant in the organizations and a performance feedback system helps people deliver on their work promises to their team, their boss and their customers. However, the biggest pressure point for assuring accountability is in the selection and oversight of the CEO.

Reflection

Should your board be having more discussion regarding the organizational culture?

Does your board get sufficient data to assure the culture and values you believe are important are alive in your organization's work culture?

Candid Considerations for Leading Volunteers

Most of your organizations use volunteer help in some capacity or other beyond the board of directors. Committees and task forces require us to tap into our constituency for talent and help. There are also many other forms of volunteer service from help with meetings to reaching out to our customer, members or constituents. Many community boards depend upon volunteer help to fulfill their mission.

The recruitment and oversight of volunteer help can be fulfilling as well as troublesome. What follows are a few guidelines that might help you upgrade the selection and oversight of your volunteers.

Not everyone qualifies. Including volunteers is not missionary work. This is business and volunteers should be carefully screened and selected, as if they were getting a job offer from you which they are. Simple yet formal applications, nominations, and interviews help ensure you select the right person for the right job. Committee volunteers require more screening than "focus group" volunteers. Create a Volunteer Application that asks volunteers to spell out their experience, leadership and specific interest in the mission of your organization. If they are interested in governance have them speak to their governance experience and competencies.

Job descriptions. As with employees, clear expectations drive performance of volunteers. Indicate the nature of the assignment they're applying for, the time investment required, and any other requirements and processes that may be relevant. This simple step weeds out the ones who are only after a quick resume entry. Make sure to disclose that volunteers must be "bondable" and will undergo a background check.

Commitment to serve. Always have volunteers sign the job description contract and a "conflict of interest" statement. Volunteers should also attest to understanding the requirements of the appointment and term of service. It's hard to fire a volunteer with no contract; it's made easier and more objective with this contract up front. Every contract should have a renewal date requiring re-appointment by the organization.

Development. Volunteers are making an investment in your organization and you need to make an investment in them. Some governance, leadership or personal development should take place at every meeting: read and discuss an article, have a short presentation, examine some aspect of governance or leadership skill. Opportunities at conferences and meetings should also include training and development: managing an agenda, Robert's Rules of Order, facilitator skills, ethics (such as, conflict of interest), policy based governance, strategic thinking. Not only do you reap immediate value, you also are preparing the succession pool for higher order committee and board service.

High caliber chairpersons and volunteer leaders. Leading volunteers can often seem like herding cats. Even the best-laid plans will encounter challenge and resistance from volunteers on occasion. You need volunteer leaders who are a mix between Mother Theresa and General Patton and have the competencies to match. Giving these volunteer leaders a bit more leadership development pays dividends in gaining great volunteer outcomes.

Refine your volunteer talent search. Waiting for the volunteer to volunteer is risking mediocrity. Organizational leaders should constantly be on the lookout for good talent and recruit as if the future of your organization depends on it--because it does. What's your process for identifying and encouraging new volunteers? How many personal "asks" have been offered to potential volunteers—this interaction is crucial to recruiting great volunteers.

Self-assessment. Creating a simple annual self-assessment tool for volunteers to use helps maintain the focus on the behaviors you desire.

These should be individual as well as group or committee wide. Individual assessments are seen by only the Chair; committee assessments, conducted anonymously, are seen by everyone. Keeping performance and expectations in focus helps lead volunteers more smoothly. These assessment results, rolled up for all committees, help provide direction to any educational efforts you may undertake.

Orientation. All highly complex equipment benefits from a quality installation. Volunteers are no different. Having a written volunteer guide that provides history and reference detail on the organization, the board and the committees assures historical perspective. Putting an up-to-date strategic plan and other background reading in the volunteer orientation packet is also critical. Maybe consider a "buddy system" connecting a new volunteer with an experienced mentor to shepherd orientation.

Rules of Engagement. The job description outlines the functions and performance requirements volunteers will be expected to fulfill. The rules of engagement describe the interpersonal approach you expect of those who are selected to serve. [Reference the "Boards of Directors Rules of Engagement" in the Support Materials section]

Recognition. Service awards, certificates, and public mention are the old standbys of recognition. Consider taking your recognition program a bit farther by sending letters to employers thanking the volunteer for their service, and having a press release template at every meeting so volunteers can send them right out to press and newsletter sources. Also send two certificates or service awards: one to the employer to pass on to the volunteer (for their office), and one for the volunteer's home or files. These small additions don't cost much but do expand the perceived value of recognition beyond the traditional. Please, no computer signatures. Little touches are noticed by your volunteers and you can certainly afford a few hundred autographs a year.

CHAPTER 9

Governance and Professional Membership Associations

Associations are complex mixes of pride, emotion, and competition for member value. Governing or managing an Association has never been easy. Today it's even more challenging thereby raising the ante for the importance of high performance governance. According to the BoardSource 2010 "NonProfit Governance Index," which reflects the impact of the economy and competition for member dollars on board decisions, 41 percent of non-profits cut or froze staff, 29 percent eliminated staff positions, 28 percent dipped into organizational reserves, and 26 percent downsized operations or reduced services. Clearly, the new normal is taking its toll in the association market space.

Dilemmas in Association Leadership

Elected boards of membership associations come replete with the leadership challenges of all democracies. Popular vote can drive some quite diverse motivations and capabilities to office. In professional associations these motivations frequently stir up turmoil over the tiniest of issues and magnify competency and personality dysfunction.

In the recent past I've personally witnessed these samples of board behavior: a board member violating the confidentiality agreement to get early news to their social network; a caste system of old school association board leadership ostracizing a new board member deemed unworthy of the sophistication of the others; a board member repeatedly calling the CEO attempting to direct management under the guise of "just sharing some insights." I could add to the list the known alcoholic rising to chairperson and embarrassing the entire association, the cancelling of board dinners because of adolescent tension across the group, the board chair and CEO affair that seemed not to bother other board members, the new chair lavishing spending on board gifts and her own personal travel that no member would ever approve.

From whence do these dilemmas evolve?

Associations are mini-cultures of larger society, so known ills should be expected. However, associations are also at risk because:

Membership is personal. Your profession is your identity. Ego and emotion drive self-preservation. Protecting status and economic vitality is anthropological, not evil. Therefore clicks, clashes and heated exchanges can be expected.

It's voluntary. Ascending to leadership positions depends on good people stepping up and frequently the best leaders don't.

It's popularity-driven. How well you're known and your personal brand are often more important in ascending to leadership than leadership competencies. Simply chairing a few committees or volunteering with your Political Action Committee does not automatically make you governance-competent. Unfortunately, service sometimes speaks louder than leadership competency and impact.

It's changing drastically. Generational tectonic plates are pushing at traditional values and ways of doing business. Membership is a commodity, participation is less of a value, employers are dropping support, learning is readily available from multiple sources, everyone's pocketbook is more competitive, and the Millennials appear to find family and free time more important than association participation.

It's frequently boring. Traditional meetings and learning sessions are giving way to "events" rather than business meetings, action learning rather than death by PowerPoint™, and virtual networking vs the annual gala.

It's magnified at the local or regional level. At this level, even less experienced leadership frequently guides the boards and committees.

Enhancing Association Governance

There are several actions an association can take to weight the odds toward competent leaders seeking board election. While none leads to a guarantee of governance quality, some at least address initiatives that can be taken that are likely to move the odds in favor of competency over popularity.

First, create a robust leadership succession learning curriculum. Expose those expressing interest in future leadership to the realities of good governance.

Start at the local level, where we first see the passion and commitment for leadership engagement appear. If associations provide a rigorous governance leadership development investment throughout their grass roots feeder system, the odds greatly increase that leaders who climb the national ladder have a chance to understand real governance. And, the association benefits from greater effectiveness on the ground while investing in the national leadership future.

Leadership development is one of the most common interests of professional membership constituencies, so there is a natural opportunity upon which to capitalize. Make "effective governance" a staple of all leadership curricula. Surprisingly, members will seek it out not simply because of their association leadership interest but also because of their community and workplace leadership interests.

Change your bylaws to require some standard curriculum on governance of candidates' choosing before running for any board—local, regional or national. At the local level, the curriculum would be the most common basics of good business governance. At the regional and national level, the curriculum would reflect the increasingly complex challenges of organizational governance of a larger enterprise. Most professionals are quite accustomed to continuing education as a means of signaling their ongoing competency, so are less prone to resist this type of "competency assurance" approach to their own association's governance.

Make a special investment in understanding the association participation of your younger members and what initiatives you may need to undertake to engage them. They are your future and they bring incredibly creative ideas to some of your endemic challenges.

Three additional perspectives may be helpful as you change the conversation about association member engagement and leadership: (1) Economic value of member leadership engagement; (2) Professional association responsibility levels of commitment to constituency leadership; (3) Governance leadership development across the lifecycle of association leader engagement.

First: what's the value of a member leader's time (see Table 11)? While these are only my estimates, my clients confirm they are reasonable economic value figures for levels of leadership engagement.

What's the message? National governance leadership should be valued at the same level as you value your legal advisor and therefore is deserving of substantial effort to assure governance competency.

TABLE 12

Valuing Constituent Engagement

Constituent Engagement Level	Economic Value
Volunteer service @ hourly support (registration desk, conference support, other coordination)	$40–$50/hr.
State committee / task force service	$75–$100/hr.
Local chapter / state board service	$250/hr.
National committee/task force	$500/hr.
National board	$500/hr.

TABLE 13

Valuing Constituent Engagement

Constituent Engagement Level	Economic Value
A one-day state chapter board meeting of nine members.	$18,000 of intellectual value; plus travel.
A seven-session, five-person national committee meeting of 1.5 hours and 3 hrs. preparation.	$11,250 of intellectual value; plus travel and staff support.
A one-day national board meeting of 11 members with 4 hours preparation.	$66,000 of intellectual value; plus travel and staff support.

Second: associations should talk openly about the robust levels of support and investment a national board should be making in developing association leadership--from the most basic professional support to the member to the national political scene.

The National Board of Directors should:

- Lead national advocacy for profession.
- Assure an association leadership pipeline.
- Support and develop State and Regional excellence.
- Rally local and regional advocacy for the profession.

State and Regional Boards should:

- Rally local and regional advocacy for the profession.
- Develop engagement in association leadership within the membership.
- Help assure continuing professional competence through professional education.
- Support members in personal advocacy in the workplace and professional advocacy in the region.

Third: from the earliest engagement of a volunteer leader, the association should have a distinct model curriculum that will support them all the way through gaining national governance leadership competency if they choose [Table 14]. Of course, all offerings should be continuing education credit eligible.

TABLE 14

Governance Leadership Development Across Lifecycle of Member Engagement in Leadership

Levels of Engagement from State to National	Educational Activity Targeted at the State Level	State/National Educational Activity of Association	National Level Educational Activity of Association	National Board Governance Support
State volunteer prospects Active volunteers	Skill training: advocacy, meeting management, finance; basic governance self-study tools. Governance workshops at all meetings.	Develop offerings and provide faculty and self-study materials.	"Leadership competency" development (typical leadership competencies + advocacy).	
State task force or committee State board potential candidates State board member	Advanced governance self-study tools available. Advanced governance workshops at all national meetings.	Advanced governance and facilitator training: self-study, workshops, mentoring.	Elected leaders "Governance Boot Camp." Governance workshops available at all national meetings.	
National association engagement interest National board interest			Advanced governance training available (virtual study + workshops).	
National / regional leader National board director			Declared board candidates required to take governance continuing education credits to qualify.	Self-assessment and tune-ups annually drive learning.

Reflection

Is your board tracking the shifting member value proposition and adjusting in a timely manner?

Does your association reach governance and leadership development all the way down to the earliest volunteer experience of a member?

How might you easily "pre-certify" governance literacy and competency for members choosing to run for state or national board positions?

CHAPTER 10

Support Materials

Contents

Role of the Chairperson in High Performance Governance

Congratulations! You're now the chairperson, contemplating becoming chairperson or wishing to push your current chairperson to improved responsibility. Whatever your motivation, a review of the crucial responsibilities of the board chairperson will be helpful.

Let's set some leadership context first. The chairperson role is a delicate balance of servant leadership and voice for accountability. Servant leadership is not "I am the smartest one leadership." You serve at the pleasure of other board members and must be inclusive with your leadership, responsive to their needs, accepting of where they are yet are a force for moving them forward. You must facilitate civil yet deep dialogue on crucial topics and help the board stay focused on the vital few important issues at each meeting. Servant leaders are always prepared, appreciative of all board views and good coaches to the board and individual members. When board or individual board member performance slacks, the chair must be the voice of accountability.

You'll find many articles and book chapters on the chairperson's role for the deeper study that may be needed, particularly if your board has unique issues. Overall, there are seven domains for chairperson leadership:

1. Facilitating and driving high performance governance.
2. Assuring the board calendar of duties.
3. Agenda setting with the executive committee and CEO.
4. Committee accountability.
5. CEO or Executive communication and coordination.
6. Meeting management and facilitation.
7. Ambassador, advocacy and public relations responsibilities.

Facilitating and driving high performance governance

The chair and vice chair should be a unified voice around developing and sustaining high performance governance. Assuring a yearly plan for board assessment and development is one means of fulfilling this responsibility. It's helpful to have the vice-chairperson lead the board assessment duties with the

187

both of you paying attention to the board's governance literacy and elements of good governance. Governance is so crucial and transparent that having board development and growth goals in the strategic plan is now commonplace.

Assuring the board calendar of duties

Every board needs a disciplined cycle of accomplishment. From elections, financial audits, self-assessment and planning it helps for the Chair to assure there is a published annual calendar of meetings for the year and the seasonal issues that surface as you move through your fiscal year. See the sample calendar in Chapter 3 for an example.

Agenda setting with the executive committee and CEO

Here's where a lot of board chairs don't demonstrate servant leadership. Trying to control the agenda single-handedly is poor leadership. Board agendas are neither the chair's nor the CEO's lone responsibility. Board agendas belong to the board and to assure they address what the board believes needs to be addressed they should be built by the executive committee. Typically the chair and CEO draft a proposed agenda and the executive committee finalizes it. This assures inclusive attention rather than autocratic agenda-setting. In today's electronic world this process is not complicated.

Committee accountability

The chair must watch committee performance closely to assure proper diligence and quality work. Partnering with the vice-chair provides an opportunity to discuss perceptions of committee work and to step in and coach when committees falter. Don't be afraid to change committee assignments if necessary. Having board members rotate committee assignments is a good board development strategy.

CEO or Executive communication and coordination

The chair is the prime link between the board and the executive team. Regular, open communication with the CEO assures that issues are identified and addressed in a timely manner and that understanding is maintained.

While I know several chairs who call the CEO several times a week, this is not likely a scenario most chairs will need unless they're under attack by the regulators or executing a merger. A once a week check-in may even be overkill. However, a once a month meeting is a good idea. Let the CEO set the agenda. It's even better if the CEO and COO (or other key deputy) and the chair and vice-chair can meet once a month. This level of partnership also contributes to succession planning.

Meeting management and facilitation

Managing meetings is the most hands-on and delicate of all the chairperson's duties. Meeting management generally falls into three categories of effort: (1) assuring fiduciary responsibility; (2) facilitation; (3) a parliamentarian role.

The fiduciary role means proper convening and proper recording of the meetings. These are the legal proceedings of a corporate board; attending to confirming attendance, agenda and decision records is a legal responsibility. A good secretary certainly carries the bulk of this burden, but the chair must keep a close eye on these details.

Facilitation is not easy. Involving quieter members, keeping dialogue on track, assuring everyone gets their point of view expressed and dealing with bullies and folks who can't stop talking make for an interesting rodeo. Keeping an eye on the processes of inclusion to assure balanced input, generative dialogue to assure full exploration of board perception and sensing consensus and moving to decision all require sensitivity as well as assertiveness. The days of the bombastic chair are ending quickly because boards are becoming smarter about their shared governance role and are refusing to be bullied by a chair. In my work with over 300 boards I've seen bullies, drunks, egotists, hand wringers and autocrats. Just because someone got elected chair does not mean they are ready for duty. Any board having an issue with the chair's behavior must take advantage of an annual self-assessment as a channel to bring this to the surface.

More difficult, the chair must bear the burden of shutting down long winded speeches, pulling the focus on conversation back to the issues at hand

189

and calling for attention when email and texting get out of hand during a meeting. For these duties it helps to have board "rules of engagement" as detailed in the Support Materials section of this book. These ground rules are ones the whole board endorses thereby giving the chair a bit more clout when holding people accountable.

Ambassador, advocacy and public relations responsibilities.

The chair is most certainly called upon to represent the board at professional meetings, government relations conferences and other public relations duties where the CEO may need chair clout. A good chair will help find opportunities for other board members to take on some of the less intense ambassador and PR duties as a means of board development but also to protect the chair's time.

Board Job Description and Commitment to Serve

As a Director of [organizational entity] I fully commit to the mission and pledge to fulfill my duties and responsibilities to carry out this mission as follows:

1. **Global Representation:** I commit to represent the broad interests of the organization's constituents rather than a narrow personal or professional perspective or special interest. I understand I am expected to know, support and follow the mission, purpose, goals and policies of the organization at all times.

2. **Board Development:** I commit to participate in ongoing board development customarily consisting of episodic presentations at regular board meetings, readings and study over the course of a year (20 to 40 hours), and participate in an annual board development and planning retreat (approximately two days). I commit to stay literate regarding the trends in the field and the performance expectations of boards of directors. I further commit to continued learning about [organizational entity] policies, programs, operations, finances and challenges and opportunities. I will participate in new board member orientation and complete the required governance continuing education required prior to my first board meeting.

3. **Due Diligence:** I will attend board meetings (schedules determined annually), special board meetings (called as needed) and be available for phone consultation (on average 20 hours annually) as needed. I will familiarize myself with the agenda and background materials sent in advance (on average, two to five hours preparation per meeting) and participate actively in the conduct of the meeting. My meeting participation should demonstrate respect for diversity of opinion, full disclosure of related information, and

adherence to rules of decision making as determined by board by-laws. I further commit to performing the duties of board membership responsibly and ethically, and to respect the confidentiality of issues of a sensitive nature brought before the board. I understand I am not to represent the board's positions to outside bodies without prior approval. I understand I am expected to support the decisions of the Board of Directors and provide dissent and questioning in private.

4. **Fiduciary Responsibility:** I understand I am expected to be literate in organizational finance and capable of tracking and evaluating financial performance through regular reports from management. I currently have or will develop competence in judging annual budgeting processes and be ready to accept accountability for the successful financial performance of the organization. I understand the fiduciary responsibilities of a board member. I understand I am expected to exercise prudence regarding personal expenses related to board business, travel or other assignments. I have signed the attached "conflict of interest" policy governing decision-making where I may face personal gain. I understand [organizational entity] may conduct a background check to assure I am bondable.

5. **Committee, Task Force, and Organizational Representation:** I understand I will be expected to serve on committees and, or, task forces. This service may require two to five hours of effort per month. I recognize Board members may also be called upon to represent the organization to internal and external constituents for special projects, negotiation, planning or communication purposes.

6. **Officers:** I understand elected board officers may face additional time commitments to those listed above.

7. **Removal**: If I am not able to meet my obligations as a board member I will offer my resignation. I understand I may expect feedback about performance on the governing body from the Chairperson and, or, Executive or Governance Committee as part of the board's annual self-assessment. I understand if I do not consistently meet expectations and commitments for board service I may be removed for cause by action of the Executive or Governance Committee. I understand overall board performance and my individual contributions may be assessed annually and improvement goals established for follow-up commitments.

BOARD OF DIRECTORS CONFLICT OF INTEREST
Statement and Form

In their capacity as directors, the members of the board of directors (the "board") of Signature Resources Inc. (hereafter referred to as "the corporation") must act at all times in the best interests of the corporation. This policy describes what constitutes a conflict of interest, guides the board in identifying and disclosing actual and potential conflicts, and helps ensure the avoidance of conflicts of interest where necessary. This policy may be enforced with individual board members as described below.

Board members have a fiduciary duty to conduct themselves without conflict to the interests of the corporation. In their capacity as board members, they must subordinate personal, individual business, third-party, and other interests to the welfare and best interests of the corporation. **A conflict of interest is a transaction or relationship which presents or may present a conflict between a board member's obligations to the corporation and the board member's personal, business or other interests.**

Definition of Terms

A financial conflict of interest is defined as: association with another entity including but not limited to for-profit or non-profit organizations or organizations that work in the corporation's field of business where a grant, stipend, salary, royalty, intellectual property right, consulting fee, honorarium, ownership interest (like stocks, stock options or other ownership interest, excluding diversified mutual funds) or other financial benefit is expected or received. These benefits are typically given to employees, managers, independent contractors (including contracted research), consultants, speaker, lecturers, faculty, advisory committee, or board members.

A fiduciary conflict of interest is defined as: interests in another organization with overlapping interests and, or, in conflict with the mission and interests of the corporation. This includes but is not limited to organizations that engage in activities that might compete or collaborate with the corporation, preventing the individual in question from fulfilling his/her responsibilities to both organizations in an impartial manner. Individuals affected by this might hold voluntary or compensated leadership positions and/or non-compensated consultancies in other for-profit or non-profit organizations or other organizations working in the corporation's field of business.

An intellectual capital conflict of interest is defined as: an association with another entity including but not limited to for-profit or non-profit organizations that could profit from exposure to the corporation's proprietary intellectual capital regarding strategy, tactics, concept or proposal documents, or whose access to such intellectual capital could compromise the corporation's proprietary position.

Recusal refers to the act of abstaining from participation in discussions, votes or any other board action due to a conflict of interest.

Full disclosure

The corporation requires the full disclosure of actual or perceived conflicts of interest both prior to initial selection for the board and on an annual basis (prior to its December board meeting) using the attached "Conflict of Interest Disclosure Form."   Situations that must be disclosed include financial, fiduciary and intellectual capital interests that compromise the individual's ability to act in the best interests of the corporation. These include financial, fiduciary, and intellectual capital relationships that have occurred in the past 12 months, and those affecting the board member's employers, colleagues, employees, or immediate family members, including spouses, partners, daughters, or sons.

For prospective board members

The corporation's policy on conflict of interest and the required annual disclosure form are not intended to dissuade qualified candidates from service to the organization. Each individual's special interests and involvements can enhance his/her ability to better serve the organization. However, when the potential for a conflict of interest exists, it is appropriate that the relevant facts be fully disclosed.

If a prospective board member currently holds a position with another for-profit or non-profit organization deemed of possible conflict with the corporation, and is asked to join the corporation's board that individual must relinquish his/her membership with that entity if elected.

By accepting an invitation to join the corporation's board, the prospective board member agrees that during the term of service, he/she will not accept candidacy for a leadership position with a competing for-profit or non-profit organization or other entity working in the corporation's field of business.

For existing board members

Based on the disclosures provided by individual board members, the board, with the support and consultation of the President or CEO, is responsible for identifying and resolving all actual and perceived conflicts of interest. Any actual or perceived conflicts of interest that arise between annual disclosures must be put in writing by the board member at the time of discovery and brought to the attention of the President or CEO.

Once a question of conflict arises, the President or CEO will bring it to the attention of the board for discussion, with all parties given the opportunity to state why they believe a conflict does or does not exist. The final decision on whether the individual has a conflict of interest will be made by a majority vote of the full board of directors. Likewise, the full board of directors will determine whether the nature of the conflict of interest requires that the individual recuse him/herself from related discussions or votes, or whether the conflict requires the individual to resign from the corporation's board.

Recusal

In cases where an individual is found to have a conflict of interest on a specific issue, the board may ask the individual to recuse him/herself from discussions and voting on all related matters. The individual must also ensure that third parties with whom they interact concerning that issue are aware they are not acting on behalf of the corporation. In most situations, no further action would be required. However, in some instances the nature of the conflict of interest may be found to be so substantive that the individual would be asked to either discontinue the activity resulting in the conflict or resign from his/her position with the corporation's board.

All conflicts of interest are not necessarily prohibited or harmful. However, full disclosure of all actual and potential conflicts, and a determination by the disinterested board or governing committee members is required. A board member must recuse themselves during a conflict of interest consideration and decision.

Notification

All actual and potential conflicts of interests shall be disclosed by board members to the governance committee through the annual disclosure form and/or whenever a conflict arises. The disinterested members of the governance committee shall make a determination as to whether a conflict exists and what subsequent action is appropriate (if any). The committee shall inform the board of such determination and action. The board shall retain the right to modify or reverse such determination and action, and shall retain the ultimate enforcement authority with respect to this policy.

On an annual basis, all board members shall be provided with a copy of this policy and required to complete and sign the acknowledgment and disclosure form below. All completed forms shall be provided to and reviewed by the governance committee, as well as any or all other conflict information provided by board members.

I attest I have read the "Signature Resources Inc. Board Conflict of Interest Policy" set forth above and agree to comply fully with its terms and conditions at all times during my service as a board member of the corporation. If at any time following the submission of this form I become aware of any actual or potential conflicts of interest, or if the information provided below becomes inaccurate or incomplete, I will promptly notify the board in writing.

Disclosure of actual or potential conflicts of interest:

_____

_____

_____

_____

_____

_____

Board Member Signature: Printed Name:

_____

Date:

Consent Agendas

Every board wrestles with the issue of agenda efficiency. Standing agenda items (staff reports, updates, etc.) frequently drag conversations off target and into the weeds (details) and expend agenda time that may be better applied to strategy or deliberation of more serious issues. **Consent agendas are one way to liberate meeting time for more valuable dialogue** (BoardSource, 2006).

A consent agenda groups routine items and resolutions under one agenda umbrella that gets received and approved in one board action without discussion. Board members who feel some aspect of the consent agenda may require discussion can move to pull that item out for more formal consideration. Any items for board action, such as a committee recommendation, should be entered on the agenda as a business decision item. Because the consent agenda can be digested mostly as pre-meeting reading and quick board action, board time is saved.

The consent agenda is frequently one of the very first actions of a convened board. Some boards decide to approve and accept the consent agenda electronically prior to the meeting. Items that most frequently qualify for a consent agenda include: committee and previous board minutes, office reports, routine correspondence, minor changes in procedure or policy (e.g. "email" is added as an acceptable method of communication to announce a meeting change), updates of documents (e.g. address changes, standard signature approval changes).

Consent agenda use requires that board members receive support materials for review well in advance of a meeting. That way they can digest material and seek follow-up information so as not to bog down precious board face-to-face time. When constructing the consent agenda the board chair and CEO need to pay attention to only items that are suitable for mechanical processing. Board members need to pay attention so that debatable issues do not inadvertently pass through without appropriate deliberation.

Board Meeting Rules of Engagement

- Get to the point, no speeches or long stories.
- Be prepared, participate.
- Be open-minded; have a sense of appreciative inquiry.
- Lighten up—not everything is an emergency or life or death.
- Focus on the problem, not the person.
- Limit side conversations, texting and emailing. Step out if you must chat or take a call.
- Pick your fights: focus on important points and don't nit pick.
- Support the decision…move on when the group moves on.
- Explore the minority opinion and encourage different points of view.
- Say it in the room, not in the hall.
- Don't rush decision-making.
- Lob up ideas or suggestions (i.e.: "how about this?" vs. "I think").
- Slay sacred cows by challenging assumptions, honoring skepticism and questioning.

Governance as Team Work

Team Support Behaviors

- Work with the ideas of others to find effective and efficient answers and strategies.
- Deal in solutions and options rather than focusing on criticism.
- Take personal initiative for working out problems with other team members.
- Frequently check team agreement and commonality of focus.
- Stay focused on relevant issues and problems.
- Support other team members during difficult times.
- Encourage and support others in team discussions.
- Ask for assistance, clarification, or information when in need.
- Stick with difficult positions and ideas objectively to ensure breadth of thought.

Board of Directors Rules of Engagement

Preparation and Participation in Board Meetings

- Complete pre-reading and background work to understand agenda items.
- Contribute to dialogue and deliberation with concise and focused comments.
- Challenge assumptions and ask the hard questions.
- Make the "business case" with your contributions, not simply opinion.
- Pick your battles; not everything is worth a tussle.
- Remain open-minded; approach topics and differences with a sense of inquiry.
- Explore minority opinion and value all points of view.
- Avoid zingers and distracting side conversations.
- Say it in the Boardroom not the hallway: we're a team and need candidness.
- Stick to lay language and avoid jargon and acronyms.
- Encourage and involve quieter members.
- Actively support group decisions. Move on when the group moves on.
- Assure discussion includes strategic relevance of all decisions.
- Stay out of the weeds and details of operations.
- Require invited presenters to submit "pre-read" materials to protect discussion time.

Ambassador Duties of Board Members

- No one speaks for the board unless authorized to represent a viewpoint/position.
- When at conferences or events remember you're ambassadors 24 hours a day.
- Consume little or no alcohol while on ambassador duty.

- Anticipate issues, questions, and materials you might need for outside meetings.
- Accept all feedback with respect, diplomacy and graciousness; report to Chairperson promptly.
- Follow-up in a timely manner if you've promised to do so.
- Be alert for future leaders who might be interested in board and committee work.
- Be on time and stay late: these are valuable opportunities for our board and organization.
- Support board positions and be prepared for the disgruntled constituent.
- Others notice how you treat staff—be respectful.

Sample Governance Committee Charter

Purpose

The Governance Committee regularly assesses board performance. It considers the board's structure, composition, operations and integrity to ensure the highest quality of governance to safeguard the organization's future. The Governance Committee also conducts the annual board nominating process and identification and facilitates recruitment of new board members.

Reporting and Staffing

The Governance Committee reports directly to the board. Any formal policy or nomination recommendations developed by the committee are advanced to the full board by the committee chair at a time and process defined by the board chair. The board chairman and CEO (or his or her designee) shall serve the committee by providing information, context and perspective and may also serve as secretary for the committee records, follow up on administrative tasks and logistical coordination.

Responsibilities

Specifically, in consultation with the board chair and CEO, the Governance Committee performs the following functions:

- Regularly **assesses the performance** of board committees, board members and the board as a whole.

- **Reviews and updates the board's policy guidelines and practices** including but not limited to conflicts of interest, confidentiality and job descriptions for board members, and committee charters and use of task forces.

- **Assesses current and anticipated needs** for board composition (competencies, experience, geography, diversity and constituencies).

- **Conducts succession planning for board leadership,** including recommending individuals for election as officers.

- Designs and oversees a process of **board orientation** for new members.

Composition, Selection and Terms

- The committee is chaired by a board member.

- The committee consists of three to four persons, a majority of whom must be board members.

- To the extent possible, committee members shall reflect the diversity of the organizational constituencies, size and geographic location.

Board Self Assessment Policy

The Board of Directors shall perform a self-assessment survey annually to evaluate critical competencies of the board and the performance effectiveness of governance functions.

Responsibilities: the "Governance Committee" is charged with the execution of the annual self-assessment and may use outside resources as approved by the board as a whole.

Timing: on or about every fourth year the board will conduct a full-scale survey of governance performance. In other years the board may focus self-assessments on specific processes (e.g., nominations, meetings, strategic planning, CEO evaluation, etc.) or other issues critical to effective governance (e.g., desired board makeup, financial literacy, board leadership succession).

Followup: annual self-assessments shall result in a board development plan to address issues determined to be high priority by the board as a whole.

Personal Assessment of Governance Contributions

1. **I feel like other board members respect my views and opinions.**

1	2	3	4	5
Not Respected		Adequately Respected		Highly Respected

2. **I feel I ask all the questions I need to ask.**

1	2	3	4	5
Don't Ask		Ask Some		Ask All I Want

3. **I feel comfortable disagreeing with other board members and staff members.**

1	2	3	4	5
Uncomfortable		OK		Very Comfortable Disagreeing

4. **I get all the information about the organization I need to make good decisions.**

1	2	3	4	5
Not much Info.		Adequate Info.		Ample Information

5. **I get to speak up as much as I want.**

1	2	3	4	5
Don't Speak Up Much		Speak Up On Occasion		Speak Up As Much as I need

6. **I completely understand my role and responsibilities as a board member.**

1	2	3	4	5
Confused		Basically Understand		Clear Understanding

7. **I review and digest board materials and come well prepared to each board meeting.**

1	2	3	4	5
Not prepared		Mostly Prepared		Well Prepared

8. **I feel the board takes on the tough issues of organizational leadership.**

1	2	3	4	5
Not usually		Most of the Time		All the Time

9. **I am able to explain our core programs and services, and their value, to those outside our board.**

1	2	3	4	5
Uncertain		Some but not all		Fully confident!

10. **I feel the board behaves in a manner consistent with our "rules of engagement" for meetings.**

1	2	3	4	5
Need lots of work		Mostly Followed		Great consistency

11. I feel board members behave in a manner consistent with our "Ambassador" rules of engagement.

1	2	3	4	5
Serious Inconsistency		Mostly Followed		Great consistency

12. In order for the board to add even greater value to our meetings and board effectiveness, I suggest the following: [please offer your ideas no matter how small they may seem to you!]

13. I believe board development in the following areas would be beneficial to our governance capability: please list.

14. Any other ideas, compliments, suggestions you would like to enter into our survey review? Please list.

Board of Directors Governance Assessment

Please provide your perception of board performance on each of these questions using the following rating and response scale.

1. <u>Little or no attention</u> or recognition by the board: needs significant improvement.
2. Some attention and recognition by the board: <u>needs improvement</u>.
3. <u>Average attention</u> and recognition by the board: I can live with this.
4. Appropriate attention and recognition by the board.
5. <u>Outstanding attention</u> and recognition by the board: we're exemplary.

Board Function

Supporting and Advancing the Vision

1. The board understands and embraces our vision?

       1   2   3   4   5

2. The board uses the vision as the standard against which strategies and policy decisions are made?

       1   2   3   4   5

3. Directors assist the key management staff to understand and support the vision?

       1   2   3   4   5

Mission

4. The board understands and embraces our Mission?

       1   2   3   4   5

5. The board reviews the mission on a regular basis?

       1   2   3   4   5

Strategic Planning

6. The board ensures an effective strategic planning process is in place?

       1   2   3   4   5

7. The board focuses its attention on strategic and policy issues rather than on operational issues?

       1   2   3   4   5

8. The board makes timely strategic decisions which are responsive to trends and other changes in the environment?
    1   2   3   4   5

9. The board devotes sufficient time to strategic issues?
    1   2   3   4   5

Fiscal Oversight

10. The board understands its financial fiduciary responsibility?
    1   2   3   4   5

11. The board understands the regulatory requirements of our business?
    1   2   3   4   5

12. The board receives sufficient information to keep current on our financial condition and to make informed and prudent fiscal decisions?
    1   2   3   4   5

13. The board makes resource allocation decisions which enable our organization to advance its vision and achieve its strategic goals?
    1   2   3   4   5

14. The board approves an annual operating budget established to support the strategic plan?
    1   2   3   4   5

Programs and Services

15. The board annually reviews the spectrum of products and services to be certain they support the mission and are consistent with the strategic plan?
    1   2   3   4   5

16. The board receives adequate information on customer, member, constituent needs, expectations and satisfaction to make decisions about products, services and policies?

    1 2 3 4 5

Board / Management Partnership

17. The board ensures that a climate of mutual trust and respect exists between the board and the Chief Executive Officer?

    1 2 3 4 5

18. The board gives the Chief Executive Officer the authority and responsibility to successfully lead and manage the organization?

    1 2 3 4 5

19. The board and CEO have agreed upon how to define success for our organization and the CEO is evaluated annually based upon these criteria?

    1 2 3 4 5

20. The board seeks and respects the opinion and recommendations of staff?

    1 2 3 4 5

Board Effectiveness

Roles and Responsibilities

21. The board understands its role?
    1   2   3   4   5

22. There is an adequate job description for board members?
    1   2   3   4   5

23. Directors execute their duties consistently?
    1   2   3   4   5

24. New Directors receive a timely, formal and substantive orientation.
    1   2   3   4   5

Governance Structure

25. The structure of the board contributes to its ability to function effectively?
    1   2   3   4   5

26. Each committee has a charter that is reviewed regularly?
    1   2   3   4   5

Board Dynamics

27. There is a climate of mutual respect and trust among directors?
    1   2   3   4   5

28. There is a climate of mutual respect and trust among directors and staff?
    1   2   3   4   5

29. Directors fully participate in board discussions?

    1 2 3 4 5

30. Directors have sufficient opportunity to express themselves on issues during board discussions?

    1 2 3 4 5

31. There is a clear commitment to building consensus on issues?

    1 2 3 4 5

32. The board makes decisions based upon information and data about customer, member or constituent needs and satisfaction?

    1 2 3 4 5

33. There is effective communication between the board, its officers and the CEO?

    1 2 3 4 5

Meetings

34. Directors receive agendas and supporting materials sufficiently prior to board meetings?

    1 2 3 4 5

35. Meeting materials are complete and well organized?

    1 2 3 4 5

36. Board meetings make the most productive use of director's time?

    1 2 3 4 5

37. Sufficient meeting time is allowed for true dialogue and reaching consensus on issues?

    1 2 3 4 5

Board Makeup

38. The current board contains a sufficient range of expertise and experience to make an effective governing body representative of the organization's marketplace?

    1   2   3   4   5

39. A formal comprehensive orientation program for new directors is in place?

    1   2   3   4   5

40. Directors help identify candidates in a timely manner for future board leadership roles?

    1   2   3   4   5

Board Development

41. The board commits time for group learning experiences designed to improve effectiveness as a governing body and increase understanding of governance issues?

    1   2   3   4   5

42. Directors are encouraged to enhance their individual leadership skills?

    1   2   3   4   5

CEO Evaluation Policy

"We strongly recommend that the entire board review and approve the chief executive's salary and benefits. The board may delegate responsibility for producing recommendations and the data to back them up to a smaller group or committee of board members. However, the final compensation package should be approved by the board as a whole." BoardSource, 2010

1. Prior to the beginning of the fiscal year, the CEO and board will outline a set of measurable objectives the board can use to evaluate his/her performance at the end of the year. These objectives should be approved by the full board.

2. An annual performance evaluation and feedback process will be facilitated by the "Executive" or "Governance Committee" of the board or by an ad hoc task force. (It should not be done by the chairman of the board.) This process will be confidential to the board and CEO.

3. Each board member will be invited to complete all instruments of evaluation related to the CEO's performance.

4. The CEO will be asked to provide a written analysis of his/her own performance, including use of the board CEO evaluation tool and providing any background material s/he wishes to provide.

   Separately, the CEO should arrange for a confidential 360-degree leadership feedback survey as part of their self-assessment process.

5. The executive or governance committee should then meet to review the results of the board survey and the CEO's assessment of his/her own performance. There should be a full board discussion of the CEO's accomplishments, including a focused discussion of strengths and developmental needs. The conclusions of this discussion should be summarized in writing including: an assessment of leadership, accomplishments, and a summary of strengths and developmental needs; an overall board satisfaction rating; and development goals for the coming year.

6. The full board reviews, discusses and agrees upon the draft summary of the CEO evaluation.

7. The CEO should receive a written draft summary of the board's assessment of his/her performance. The board executive or governance committee should then meet with the CEO to discuss its conclusions. The committee should remain open to the possibility of modifying its evaluation, based upon this discussion.

8. Following the meeting with the CEO, the committee may need to meet again to modify its written evaluation. The written evaluation should then be presented to the full board in an executive session. Following discussion, the full board should vote to accept the formal evaluation.

9. The board should have a formal compensation system that ties the results of the evaluation into whatever salary increases or bonuses the CEO receives as a result of the evaluation. All board members should be fully involved regarding the salary level, salary increases and bonuses received by the CEO.

10. The final step in the process should be the development of the next year's performance objectives by the CEO and full board approval of these objectives, the formal evaluation, the compensation increases, and the CEO performance objectives for the next year.

Effective Briefings to Managers and Boards of Directors

How many of you have pitched your manager, an executive or board of directors with a suggestion? I know for many of you this is a regular event. Now, what do you believe your boss or board was thinking while listening to you? If you believe you had their full attention, you're most likely wrong. If you think they were marveling at your oral presentation skills, you are likely hallucinating. If you think they would like you to become more efficient <u>and</u> effective in your briefings, you're right!

Unless we've had a great boss who taught us how to give effective executive briefings, or, unless we've successfully mastered presentation and interpersonal skills from the numerous workshops available, most of us can most likely benefit from tuning up our reports and idea pitches to management. Here's the ugly truth about us in management or governance: we're busy! While we trust and like most of you, you don't always use our time wisely. We're too kind to tell you how frustrating it is. We've got multiple fires burning and our own manager or constituency on our back so our brain multitasks even if our physical behavior doesn't indicate it. We carry around a set of key questions (see below) we're always waiting to hear answered and appreciate those of you who come prepared to do so. We suffer through the others of you who bumble around disorganized, don't get to the point, and are frequently unprepared for the basic questions we will ask.

Boards and managers don't have time for the trivial detail or the lifetime history of a problem or idea. We like it concise, tailored to our pressures and interests, and thought out thoroughly so we can cut to the chase and get ideas on the table to consider. That doesn't mean we don't like chit chat on occasion nor that we refuse to talk you through a difficult challenge. It simply means, protect our time, pitch to our interests, and be prepared to offer your suggestions so I can see that you have thought about the topic. Here are a few direct recommendations that will help you gain credibility with management.

1. **Get to the point**. Consider every opportunity to brief or update your leadership will be cut short and **hook us with the key message within the first 90 seconds**. In communication this is referred to as your

"elevator message." If you could only talk to me in the elevator, what would you focus on for that one and a half minute ride that would most powerfully get my attention? If you're making a recommendation—begin with that and work backwards.

2. **Anticipate the key questions of leadership.** There are five: (a) Why should I listen? (b) What's your idea or key point? (c) Do you have a recommendation? (d) How does your recommendation help meet business goals, customer interests or help our workforce (dollars, customers and co-workers)? (e) What specifically do you need from me/us?

3. Be prepared to offer **detail about implementation** having thought through any potential roadblocks, challenges, or objections that might come up. At a high level give me hope your idea can work.

4. Call for the sale: make sure I **know what you need from me** and what my support would look like specifically.

6. Let me see your **passion**. Another recitation of turgid mush won't get my juices flowing!

[See also "Flip that Meeting to Improve Outcomes, Engagement and Satisfaction," in 9MinuteMentor section on www.signatureresources.com]

Executive Summaries to Executives and Boards of Directors

Making Better Business Decisions: Executive Summaries

Boards constantly struggle to focus the amount of information and decision calls they get in order to focus on only the vital few issues rather than the trivial many topics people would like to present to them. Executive summaries of reports and recommendations have become commonplace as a means of facilitating efficiency and focus.

The "executive summary" is a one page tool (two pages if you absolutely can't help yourself) that condenses recommendations and background context for focused and efficient consideration by executives and boards of directors. Consider the elements of an effective executive summary identified below.

Recommendation: Cut to the chase with a bottom line statement of what you recommend. Or, a concise statement of the dilemma or problem.

Context: Scope an opportunity statement to clearly articulate the business focus. Summarize the elements in the environment, constituent interests, threats, opportunities or benchmarking that has led to your recommendation. This might include a statement of what might happen should your recommended action not take place. Possibly an "acuity" rating: e.g., emergency, urgent, important, strategic (longer range).

Evidence/Data: Overview the evidence based data that might support your recommendation: research, confirmed damage from a decision/event, constituent interests, marketplace drivers.

Resource implications: financial, staffing, volunteer effort, partnerships, etc.

"I think I speak for all of us when I say
what in God's name are you talking about?"

Executive Summary Template

Think of an "Executive Briefing or Board Briefing"

as an Executive Summary

- A written executive summary should accompany ALL briefings to the board or organizational executives.
- The more fractious / contentious / politically sensitive the recommendation or update—then have several other pages of background to attach FYI to your executive summary.
- DO NOT READ to us. We've read it—cut to the chase and let the board or executive set the Q/A and Discussion agenda.

An effective executive summary is 1 page outlined in 3 segments:

Begin with the bottom line:

- The recommendation, or...   The current status, or...   The serious-
ness of the dilemma.

Then work backward to scope a "brief" context: anticipate the key issues of interest to the board.

- <u>High-level</u> data: $ (always financial implications to everything), his-
torical perspective / actions, survey data, positions of other key players
(associations, interest groups, businesses, thought leaders, etc.). High
level not decimal points!
- Strategic implications: how does it tie to strategic plan?
- Problem solved or advantage gained by the recommendation or action.
- Any ethical, political or legal implications?
- Key points of your deliberation, research, and benchmarks you've
used.
- Reasons for optimism.
- Historical relevance: any precedents of relevance?

FAQs

- What might be the frequently asked questions?
  - ~ You've anticipated some above with your "context points."
  - ~ Timing, prioritization, other priorities that might have to be
shifted.
  - ~ Think ahead of what might be asked.

YES, all three segments on ONE PAGE.
That's why it's called a "briefing" or "summary."

225

Dealing with Questions and Objections

To Your Briefing

Few business or professional presentations are conducted without audience interaction and question and answer exchanges. Business decision making is conducted more and more through dialogue rather than formal presentations so preparing to engage in "Q and A dialogue" with groups is helpful preparation. No matter what the occasion or formality of the situation, credible speakers enhance credibility through responses to audience questions.

Please understand that poise, honesty and conciseness are critical when dealing with questions.

Use these guidelines and strategies to maintain control and credibility during questioning:

- When you do get questions, make sure you understand them. A good way to make sure you understand and to make sure the audience has heard it too is to repeat the question in your own words.

- Answer questions as directly and as concisely as you can. If you will answer the question later in the presentation, just say so; then when you get to the point in the presentation, remind the original questioner that you are about to answer the question asked earlier.

- When answering a question requiring a bit of background first, let the audience know where you're going with your explanation then signal them when you get to the direct answer sought by the question.

- Listen carefully to questions, especially the lengthy run-on question that may be several questions in one. Focus on answering one at a time. If you forget one of the questions it's o.k. to ask, "Now what was your third question?"

- Don't give confrontational questioners the satisfaction of losing control of your emotions or diplomatic cool. If they ask a good question, tell them so. If they make a good point, admit it. Don't reinforce negative or highly charged emotional language by repeating it. Use phrases like: "I certainly wouldn't use those words" or "I disagree with your characterization of the issue."

- Hypothetical questions may be trouble. These questions frequently contain faulty assumptions and premises that you might not wish to tackle "off the cuff." If you must answer make it absolutely clear that you are "speculating" and would not be held accountable for taking a position without further study and review based on actual facts and events. Even then, recognize the dangerous territory.

- When a persistent questioner or person requiring lots of detailed response begins interfering with your ability to fulfill your objectives, reinforce that they are making inquiries deserving of proper attention and ask that they address it with you after the meeting some time. Use this approach for the filibuster question that is unfocused, rambling and run-on. Indicate your intention to talk to them later to better understand their concerns.

- Intense adversarial questions require a display of control and confidence by you as respondent. Look directly at the questioner, address them by name, thank them for raising their concern ("an important question"), move away from a central speaking position in the room and closer to the questioner, and then answer using the best combination of strategies reviewed above. Your positioning, calm tone of voice, direct use of name and "thank you" for the question will signal your confidence and control.

- If you've been interrupted by a question or questions: when you're ready to proceed with your presentation, tell the audience. Provide a quick "here's where we were" summary and then proceed. Remember: their attention has been diverted to the question and the train of thought of your answer. Bring them back.

- Pause before answering difficult or politically charged questions to give yourself time to do it right. Only you feel the pain of the pause. To the audience a reasoned pause conveys confidence and control. When you give a good answer they will not remember that you took a couple of seconds to pull it together.

Maintain control of the question and answer portion of your presentation. Be directive, diplomatic, and keep your poise. It's still your credibility on the line.

Follow-up

Don't waste any presentation regardless of its effectiveness. Take a little time following the immediate communication situation and review your performance.

- What worked well?
- What helped you feel especially comfortable?
- What did not work as well?
- What do others have to say about your presentation? Ask a valued peer for feedback.
- Glance back through the executive briefing and Q-A guidance and double check what helped and what you may have overlooked.
- Provide timely follow-up to information, materials, references or referrals promised in the presentation.

Ten Considerations if you Must Use PowerPoint™

© MARK ANDERSON, WWW.ANDERTOONS.COM

"OK, I'm now going to read out loud every single slide to you, word for word, until you all wish you'd just die."

The ubiquitous PowerPoint™ is both boon and bane. An extraordinary means of organizing material and creating custom, visually engaging materials, it's helped many a person—from fourth graders to executives—piece together their messages. Yet, who among us has not suffered through the wrong application of this dynamic organizing tool misused in a presentation—prisoner of the PowerPoint™?

It is not being a Luddite to ask each of us to think twice before using PowerPoint™ in our presentations. At least, think seriously about the missteps you may be about to make.

1. **Think again**. If you're planning to read it to us, please email it instead, cancel the meeting, and save you embarrassment and us boredom and wasted time. Nothing is less credible and disengaging than the oral reading of PowerPoint™.

2. **Cut it back**. Complex diagrams, data comparisons, graphs, and charts are always helped by a visual. Cut out the narrative and the ten bullet slides and simply talk to us using the graphs and charts to amplify your message. Don't allow critical information to be hidden deep in a busy slide.

3. **Talk to me**. Please don't turn your back and talk to the screen. Also, don't turn out the lights. Leave enough light that we can actually see you. You want us to see the star communicator of the show: is that you, or the PowerPoint™?

4. **Give us a no PowerPoint™ intro**. Build rapport with the group; let us see your personality before you glaze over our eyes with your dynamic pictures, cartoons, and outlines. We might even remember that you were there.

5. **Don't simply refer to the slides**. Tell me a story. Weave a message with your passion and crisp explanation while letting the slides amplify your messages. It's called a "visual aid;" to support your messages not a substitute for them.

6. **Simple please**. Cut the cute graphics from your kid's computer. Dump those middle school motivational pictures of mountain climbing, rapids kayaking, and eagles soaring with geese. This is business. And please, only a few points and no narratives per slide. If I can't catch it with a glance then you're taking attention away from you.

7. **Interact with me as we go**. Prisoners of the PowerPoint™ chafe leaving questions to the end. No interaction with the audience makes Jack and Jill and the presentation a dull bore. If you've ever briefed an executive you have learned you won't make it three minutes anyway without being interrupted. By engaging us as you go you can read our reaction to your message and better gauge how to amplify the on screen content.

8. **Direct the slides yourself.** Adding insult to injury is the "next slide," "no, go back a slide please" interactions with your joystick partner bent over the computer. Please learn to use the technology so you don't look like a circus act. Carry your own remote screen control device so you can always control your slides.

9. **Treat this like a real presentation not an informational memo.** These tactics are still valuable: clear thesis and purpose, overview introduction, crisp organizational flow with distinct points easily gleaned from all the content and a powerful summation and call to action. Get out that old speech book.

10. **My copy please.** There are few things worse than having to ask for a copy of your slides. Active listeners like to take notes, have a record, and feel you cared enough to really share. We also want all those references you tossed around while you spoke. And, should you mis-use the technology we like to fast forward through the slides and decide whether to stay to hear you babble on or leave and use our time more wisely. If possible, upload your presentation to the board protected area on the organizational web site. Or, if you're making a more public presentation upload to the public access site SlideShare and announce days in advance of your presentation that people can access your slides there.

Executive Summary Example

Recommendation: Priority is urgent. The Acme Board Finance Committee recommends the creation of a standing board audit committee to oversee independent assessments of organizational finance and other areas of risk. [Task force members, D. Smith, R. Aragon, F. Lagano]. It is further recommended that this committee be composed of three current board members, a past president and an outside financial expert (total = 5 members).

Context: In 2002 federal legislation known as "the Corporate and Auditing Accountability and Responsibility Act," (Sarbanes-Oxley Act) required corporations to be held to a higher standard of transparency and risk assessment. Governing bodies created audit committees independent of board financial committees or staff finance staff to comply with the intent of the law. This movement to independent risk assessment has permeated the not-for-profit sector and such audit committees are now commonplace.

Our opportunity is to create an "Audit Committee" to facilitate an independent external audit of the organization's financial health and practices, assure and support board follow through on any "exceptions" from standard accounting principles or financial transactions identified by the audit, and investigate any other organizational risk or whistleblower issues they deem important for broader risk management.

The audit committee is typically separate from the finance committee (no overlapping members), with the committee majority being board members. It is not unusual for an audit committee to have an outside voting or non-voting member with a financial background.

Evidence/Data: Creation of this committee is deemed "urgent" due to the recent findings of the new acting CFO of lapses in timely financial accounting and reconciliation. To date no unethical or fraudulent behavior has come to light. It has been discovered that past audits called attention to exceptions in financial management that had not been followed up on by the board. *BoardSource*, the pre-eminent recognized source for best governance practices in the not-for-profit world strongly recommends creation of audit committees as a standard of high performance governance. ["The Sarbanes-Oxley Act and Implications for Nonprofit Organizations" *BoardSource,* 2006]

Resource implications:

Financial/Staffing: the Board currently budgets for an external financial audit so no significant budget impact is anticipated for this line item.

Audit committees are quickly evolving into full "enterprise risk management" committees and expanding their purview to a broader range of organization risks (e.g. emergency business resumption, security, insurance coverage, IT) such that an "internal auditor" position to conduct these additional risk management assessments is anticipated within three years. Salary +/- $60,000 + benefits.

Financial: an outside financial expert for the committee (separate from the "auditing" firm) may involve some professional fees if volunteers cannot be recruited (est. $10,000/yr.).

Volunteer: board member committee service, association member service, past president service.

Support Materials: see attached recommended "Audit/ERM Committee Charter."

Sample Board Orientation Scope

New board member orientation is a combination of offsite materials review, onsite introductions and briefings and completion of four hours of governance education provided on DVD. Content may be expected as follows:

I. Offsite materials review

- History of the organization
- Mission, vision, values statements
- Summary of programs, products, services
- Newsletters, press clippings
- Financial performance for the past three years including external audit findings
- Annual Report
- Human resources organizational chart and bio-sketch professional backgrounds of staff
- Strategic Plan
- Board by-laws
- One year of board minutes
- Board policy and procedures
- Current board profile and professional background bio-sketches
- Board commitment and conflict of interest statements for signing
- Recent governance self-assessment results
- Board committee structure and charters
- Board calendar

II. Onsite introductions and briefings

- Staff leadership welcome meeting and introductions
- Key programmatic one on one meetings
- Financial briefing from CFO and review of board financial dashboard
- Human resources briefing including review of board "organizational climate" dashboard

- Constituent / customer / member briefing including last twelve months satisfaction and value survey results
- Board Chair briefing: Board composition philosophy and leadership succession
- Board committee assignment

III. Governance Education

- Digest assigned articles and booklets
- View "21ˢᵗ Century Governance" DVDs (Wallace, 2013)
- Phone consultation with Governance committee chair upon completion

Governance Leadership References

Aaker, David, "Building Strong Brands," (2011).

Bainbridge, Stephen. The New Corporate Governance in Theory and Practice (2008).

Baroudi, Richard. KPI Mega Library: 17,000 Key Performance Indicators (2010).

Beckwith, Harry. Selling the Invisible (1997).

BoardSource, Assesssment of the Chief Executive: User's Guide (2005).

BoardSource, Financial Responsibilities of Nonprofit Boards (2009).

BoardSource, NonProfit Executive Compensation (2010).

BoardSource, Nonprofit Governance Index (2012).

BoardSource. "The Consent Agenda: A Tool for Improving Governance" (2006).

Board Source, The Handbook of Nonprofit Governance (2010).

BoardSource, "The Sarbanes-Oxley Act and Implications for Nonprofit Organizations" (2006).

Board Source, Twelve Principles of Governance That Power Exceptional Boards (2005).

Bradley, Chris, et. al. "Have You Tested Your Strategy Lately?" McKinsey Quarterly (1/2011).

Brown, Jim. The Imperfect Board Member: Discovering the Seven Disciplines of Governance Excellence (2006).

Buckingham, Marcus and Curt Coffman. First Break All the Rules (1999).

Canadian Coalition for Good Governance, Building High Performance Boards (2010).

Carver, John. Boards That Make a Difference (2006).

Carver, John and Miriam Carver. CarverGuide, Basic Principles of Policy Governance (1996).

Carver, John and Miriam Carver. Reinventing Your Board (2006).

Canton, James. The Extreme Future (2007).

Chait, Richard, et. al. Governance as Leadership (2004).

Charan, Ram. Owning Up: the 14 Questions Every Board Member Needs to Ask (2009).

Coerver, Harrison and Mary Byers, "Race for Relevance: 5 Radical Changes for Associations" (2011).

Day, George and Paul Schoemaker, Peripheral Vision: Detecting the Weak Signals that will Make or Break Your Company (2006).

DailyCrowdsource. **http://dailycrowdsource.com/crowdsourcing-basics/ what-is-crowdsourcing**.

Deiser, Roland and Sylvain Newton. "Six Social-Media Skills Every Leader Needs," McKinsey Quarterly (2/2013).

Divol, Roxane, et. al. "Demystifying Social Media," McKinsey Quarterly (4/2012).

Fraser, John and Betty Simkins, Eds. Enterprise Risk Management: Today's Leading Research and Best Practices for Tomorrow's Executives (2010).

Few, Stephen. Information Dashboard Design (2006).

Frigo, Mark. "Strategic Risk Management: The New Core Competency," Balanced Scorecard Report (1/2009).

Gammel, C. David. Managing Engagement (2011).

Gluck, Frederick, et. al. "Thinking Strategically," McKinsey Quarterly (10/1978; 2000).

Gorbis, Marina. The Nature of the Future: Dispatches from the Socialstructured World (2013).

Gwin, Bonnie. "Secrets of the World's Best Boards," Heidrick and Struggles (1/2010). **www.heidrick.com**.

Hamel, Gary. Leading the Revolution (2002).

Hamel, Gary and Liisa Valikangas. "The Quest for Resilience," Harvard Business Review (9/2003).

Hauswirth, Jeff, et. al. "What Boards Get Right," Point of View: Spenser Stuart (1/2012).

Hearst, Marti. "Social Technology," http://www.slideshare.net/marti_hearst/ social-technology (2009).

Heifetz, Ronald and Donald Laurie "The Work of Leadership," Harvard Business Review (1/1997).

Hesselbein, Frances, et. al., Eds. The Organization of the Future (1997).

Ioannou, Charlie. "SWOT Analysis—An easy to understand guide" (2012).

Johansen, Bob. Get There Early (2007).

Kaplan, Robert and David Norton. Balanced Scorecare (1996).

Kaplan, Robert, et. al. "Managing Risk in a New World," Harvard Business Review (10/2009).

Kaplan, Robert and David Norton. Strategy Maps (2004).

Kiel, Geoffrey, et. al. Board Directors and CEO Evaluation (2005).

Kim, W. Chan. Blue Ocean Strategy (2005).

Kouzes, James and Barry Posner. The Leadership Challenge: How to Make Extraordinary Things Happen in Organizations (2012).

Leslie, Jean. "What you need, and don't have, when it comes to leadership talent." Center for Creative Leadership (6/2009) **http://www.ccl.org**.

Martin, James. Meaning of the 21st Century (2007).

McAfee, Andrew and Erik Brynjolfsson. "Big Data: The Management Revolution," Harvard Business Review (10/2012).

Mintzberg, Henry. "The Fall and Rise of Strategic Planning," Harvard Business Review (1/1994).

National Association of Corporate Directors, Bridging Effectiveness Gaps: A Candid Look at Board Practices (2013).

National Association of Corporate Directors, Corporate Minutes: A Director's Guide (2013).

National Center for Nonprofit Boards, The Policy Sampler: A Resource for Nonprofit Boards (2000). [Also: www.boardsource.org/QnA.asp?Category=16.]

Niven, Paul. Balanced Scorecard Step by Step by Government and Nonprofit Agencies (2008).

Office of Personnel Management. "OPM Leadership Competencies." (2013).

Petersen, John. Out of the Blue: Wild Cards and Other Big Future Surprises (1997).

PWC, Insights from the Boardroom 2012, Price Waterhouse Coopers (2012).

Ries, Al and Laura Ries. The 22 Immutable Laws of Branding (2002).

Schwartz, Peter. The Art of the Long View (1991).

Senge, Peter. The Fifth Discipline (1990).

Sladek, Sarah. The End of Membership as we Know It (2011).

Slywotzky, Adrian. Value Migration: How to Think Several Moves Ahead of the Competition (1996).

Sonnenfeld, Jeffrey, et. al. "What CEOs Really Think of Their Boards," Harvard Business Review (4/2013)

SpencerStuart. 2011 Spencer Stuart Board Index (2011).

Stavros, Jacqueline and Gina Hinrichs. The Thin Book of SOAR: Building Strengths-Based Strategy (2009).

Taleb, Nassim, et. al. "The 6 Mistakes Executives Make in Risk Management," Harvard Business Review (10/2009).

Terry, Alexis. "Next Generation and Governance," BoardSource (2008).

Thornton, Grant. 2012 National Board Governance Survey of NonProfits, Grant Thornton (2012). **www.grantthornton.com**.

Vaill, Peter. Learning as a Way of Being (1996).

Wade, Woody. Scenario Planning: A Field Guide to the Future (2012).

Wallace, Les. "9MinuteMentor Governance Series." (2013).

Wallace, Les and James Trinka. A Legacy of 21st Century Leadership (2007).

Wheatly, Margaret. Leadership and the New Science (2006).

Wiener, Edie and Arnold Brown. Future Think: How to Think Clearly in a Time of Change (2005).

Zenger, Jack and Joe Folkman. The Extraordinary Leader 2002).

CARTOONS

Anderson, Mark. www.Andertoons.com. All Andertoons cartoons are copyrighted material and used here with permission and through royalty payment. Cartoons cannot be used without permission.

Les Wallace, Ph.D.
President, Signature Resources Inc.

The Small Business Commerce Association recognized Signature Resources as a "Small Business of the Year, 2009."

Les Wallace has a Ph.D. in Communication and Organizational Behavior from the University of Oregon. He founded Signature Resources in 1982 and has grown the company into a 40 person consulting consortium of individuals and partner organizations. The Signature Resources consortium provides governance and leadership strategy and development to public and private sector enterprise globally through two domestic and three international offices. During 30 years service as a strategist to business and government Dr. Wallace has also served as university professor and administrator at the University of Oregon and Colorado State University, and hospital administrator at a large urban teaching hospital.

Dr. Wallace is recognized for tracking business environment and workplace trends and their impact upon business and government. Mixing practical solutions to today's organizational challenges with leading edge ideas Les stretches our thinking about designing our future. His workshops, seminars and speaking engagements reach 20,000 people a year. His publications have appeared in <u>Leadership Excellence</u>, <u>Personnel Journal</u>, <u>Credit Union Management</u>, <u>Leader's Digest</u>, <u>Vistage View</u>, <u>Public Management</u>, and <u>Nation's Business</u> as well as numerous research and conference proceedings. He is co-author of three business books, <u>Influence in the Workplace: Maximizing Personal Empowerment</u> (Kendall-Hunt 1992), <u>Speak With Credibility</u>™ (Signature Resources, 3ʳᵈ Ed.

2002) and <u>A Legacy of 21st Century Leadership</u> (iUniverse, 2007). His workbook, <u>21st Century Governance</u> is used by several boards of directors and about 200 board members a year for governance development. Signature Resources programs "Performance Engagement Competencies"™ teaching coaching and employee engagement skills and "Xtreme Breakthrough Performance!"™ bringing breakthrough innovation to organizations are recognized as benchmarks in the organizational performance arena.

Les is a frequent consultant and speaker on issues of organizational transformation and leadership, strategic thinking, board of directors development, governance, and coaching. His clients have included Fortune 100 businesses such as Hewlett-Packard, Dupont, Aetna, and Kodak. Government clients include the Internal Revenue Service, FBI, Nuclear Regulatory Commission, US Postal Service, and the U.S. Department of Health and Human Services as well as numerous state and local government entities. Dr. Wallace has worked with over 300 Board of Directors.

Dr. Wallace is active in the following organizations: the World Future Society, ASAE-The Center for Association Leadership, and the Credit Union Executive Society. Dr. Wallace recently served on the Board of Directors of Security First Bank in the Midwest and now serves on two boards: the Board of Counterpart International, a 40 year old global community development and humanitarian aid organization based in Washington, D.C. and the Board of the World Future Society. Les has also served on the faculty of the Institute for Global Chinese Affairs at the University of Maryland and the FBI Academy Law Enforcement Executive Development Seminar.

Les@signatureresources.com   **303-680-7555**

THE **NineMinute** MENTOR ADVANTAGE

Content Advantages for Your Professional Association:

High quality learning with minimal time commitment.
Provide hundreds of learners quality content at pennies per view.
Integrate the content into existing or new member value offerings.
Scalable application from novice to seasoned board member.
Scalable involvement from independent to group learning.
Concise, focused tutorials create opportunity for immediate application.
View again and again to refresh your governance perspective.

Join These Organizations Already Training Their Boards:
American Nurses Association
Mountain States Credit Union Association
Oncology Nursing Society
Board of Certification for Athletic Trainers/Nat. Athletic Trainers Association
American Association of Nurse Anesthetists
Counterpart International

9Minute Mentor Governance Series available for immediate utilization.

For Preview Access Contact: Les Wallace
Les@signatureresources.com